D0633542

# THINK HOME

# THINK HOME

everything you need to plan and create your perfect home

**JUDITH WILSON**

*photography by* Polly Wreford

LONDON • NEW YORK

First published in 2014 by
Ryland Peters & Small
20–21 Jockey's Fields,
London WC1R 4BW

and

519 Broadway, 5th Floor
New York, NY 10012
www.rylandpeters.com

10 9 8 7 6 5 4 3 2 1

Senior designer
Paul Tilby

Commissioning editor
Annabel Morgan

Location research
Jess Walton

Production manager
Gordana Simakovic

Art director
Leslie Harrington

Editorial director
Julia Charles

Text © Judith Wilson 2014
Design and photography
© Ryland Peters & Small 2014

The author's moral rights have been asserted. All rights reserved. No part of this publication may be reproduced, stored in a retrieval system or transmitted in any form or by any means, electronic, mechanical, photocopying or otherwise, without the prior permission of the publisher.

ISBN 978 1 84975 504 7

A catalogue record for this book is available from the British Library.
US Library of Congress cataloging-in-publication data has been applied for.

Printed and bound in China

# CONTENTS

# INTRODUCTION:
# WISHFUL THINKING

**OPPOSITE** This seemingly simple room exudes clever planning. Note the echoes between the hat in the photograph and the coolie lampshade, plus the ribbed textures of the rug and the linen upholstery.

Designing a beautiful, well-balanced home begins with wishful thinking. Our prevailing culture is to dive right in; act first, think second. But isn't it better to sit back and dream, compose, reflect, evaluate and imagine, all before designing or changing a thing? Design experts agree that careful contemplation at the start leads to a strong concept, organized planning and a seamlessly executed project delivered on time. So follow their lead. Long before starting to design, sit down with zero distractions and have a good, long, productive think.

Focused thinking crystallizes your thoughts and puts them in order, allowing you to create a targeted action plan. Clever thinking will save you money, because forethought buys time, giving you the freedom to shop around for competitive estimates or well-priced materials. Free thinking means you can tailor your home space to suit your lifestyle. Creative thinking helps you to design every centimetre of your interior so that it hangs together beautifully and looks amazing. Marshalling your thoughts is a powerful secret weapon.

Actively reflect on your thought processes. We're all adept at sketching, making to-do lists or consulting floor plans. But stretch your mind and try lateral thinking. Draw mind maps for

**ABOVE** Put smart thinking into tiny details, and play around with a deliberate mix of similarity and contrast. Here, horizontally stacked magazines echo the vertical carving on the fireplace, while the easy curves of a vintage metallic light are juxtaposed with intricate gilded mouldings.

**LEFT** The more pared down the room, the more intensive the planning required. This quiet corner is soulful, simple and minutely detailed, with ample reading materials and task lighting close to hand.

**LEFT** Adopt an experimental approach to mixing up historical periods, and do so with tongue-in-cheek boldness. Here, an antique stool looks unexpectedly dramatic in front of modern art.

**ABOVE** Enjoy contrasting shapes: straight with curvy, regimented with organic, skinny with plump.

**OPPOSITE** Take a classic motif or piece of furniture, then zip it up with acid colour. It shouldn't work, but it does.

each room, highlighting structural changes or the ambience you'd like. Apply critical thinking to nascent design ideas, dissecting them constructively with self-imposed questions. If you're co-designing with a partner, then brainstorm and opt for collaborative thinking, dovetailing varying concepts. Try 'in-a-nutshell' thinking. Can you sum up in one sentence what you're aiming to achieve at home?

You will find that wishful thinking is not an indulgence but a liberation. Dare to dream, and do so with no holds barred. How do you want your perfect home to look, feel and function? Secretly, we all know that as a project progresses certain details are lost. Starting with the big picture means that compromise will feel less painful. Once the ultimate vision is in your mind's eye, mentally add a few constraints such as low budget or working to a limited colour palette. Problem-solving often pushes creativity to the next level.

Most of us are tempted to start the design journey by gathering ideas at the outset, trawling design showrooms, magazines and blogs. These are all fantastic source of visual inspiration, but starting too soon can lead to sensory overload and ultimately become confusing. So try to do your wishful thinking before gathering real examples, then you will feel organized and ready to seize the trends that truly appeal.

**OPPOSITE** Clever planning isn't just about delivering good looks but also versatility. These metal chairs are practical and family-friendly, yet the scarlet looks chic for evening entertaining.

**BELOW** Design each area as if using a camera, zooming back and forth from full-room view to close-up. Every still life should be beautiful on its own, as well as being part of the whole.

**RIGHT** There are no right or wrong answers when it comes to playing with scale. Here, the giant flag, tiny chair and mid-scale wallpaper make a small room intriguing.

*Think Home* has been devised to stimulate your thoughts, whether you're designing a home from scratch, redoing certain rooms, adding an extension/addition or giving your living quarters a revamp. The first chapter, Think Hard, evaluates the facts, thinking through productive ways to use existing architecture, room sizes and the available budget. Next, Think Inspired helps realize the potential of your living space by looking through a 'lifestyle' lens, devising spaces according to how you like to live. Chapter 3, Think Lifestyle, is focused on inspiration – colour, texture and pattern – and how you can harness each element to create a chic, pulled-together finish. And in the final chapter, Think Rooms, thoughts turn back to individual rooms in the house, highlighting the essential features each one needs to deliver.

While wishfully thinking about how to shape your dream home and what it will look like, consider, too, what home represents to you. Is it a retreat, a family zone or a social hub? What is your philosophy for home? Add these thoughts into the mix. Think yourself into your new environment. Think mindfully. Think creatively. Think practically. Think home.

AMO

# 1 THINK HARD

diptyque 34 boulevard saint germain
JA
CIN
THE
paris 5e
JAS
MIN
MA
QUIS
paris 5e

# THINK ...ARCHITECTURAL BONES

**EXPERT THINKING**

"A stripped space is like a blank canvas. Take time to look at it and get inspired by it. See how daylight enters the room, how shadows define its form.

**KARIN DRAAIJER**
*INTERIOR DESIGNER*

**OPPOSITE** In this period home, the dominant ceiling beams provide an architectural springboard for the entire kitchen design. There is a pleasing symmetry about the mix of straight lines, with horizontal wood fascias for cupboards and vertical partitions that exactly match the width of the ceiling beams. Within this cohesive framework, there is 'breathing space' for a plain splashback and square tiled floor.

**RIGHT** A show-off fire surround can spark not one but two visual threads. With its prominent white veining, this example is the basis for a monochrome theme. Yet its ornate lines have prompted a simple, modern look for the remaining furniture. Look to architectural bones as a crucial source of contrast, too.

Think of the architecture of your home as the essential skeleton onto which you'll hang surfaces, colour and furniture. The design process should begin, therefore, with a detailed appraisal of these crucial architectural bones, both the beautiful and the nondescript, from window styles and staircases to mouldings and flooring. Start with a gut reaction. What works, and what doesn't? Then measure up to get the hard facts. Photograph key features, as there's nothing like scrutinizing visuals to see where architectural consistencies (or anomalies) lie.

If your home needs major restructuring, or you are embarking on a new-build or building an extension or addition to your home, it is smart thinking to hire an architect to help shape those critical bones. This doesn't have to cost a fortune; many architects are happy to undertake the design and drawings and to help navigate planning regulations, but not to oversee the entire project. Meet several architects, obtain competitive quotes and pick the professional whose thinking seems to be most in tune with your needs and dreams.

Whether buying new or re-evaluating an existing home, what you're looking for – and aiming to enhance – is a strong, cohesive architectural character. The symmetrical proportions of a Georgian cottage or the picture windows of a 1970s house will already have tangible design handwriting. Most homes, though, will be a composite of alterations. So identify any original features and, if possible, weed out newer additions. Stripping out stylistically inconsistent features will help the original bones shine through.

Once you've identified the strongest architectural characteristics, these will supply a visual 'hook' for the rest of your scheme. You might focus on the detailing of a distinctive panelled door or something universally prominent, like exposed timber ceiling beams, recurring throughout the property. Consider how you will

**LEFT** In a new-build home, the addition of architectural features will contour every space. Here, vertical panelling and a high ceiling draw the eye along the corridor towards a natural focal point.

**LEFT** Within this 1970s house, major alterations provided the opportunity for unexpected features. Here, a staircase is 'hidden' between bookshelves.

**OPPOSITE** When a basement conversion is added to a period property, a modern staircase can provide a physical and visual transition into the new space.

underline these architectural elements. The visual message must be clear and crisp. You can either faithfully 'copy' features, such as original window shutters, so that everything matches in every room, or choose to reinterpret a particular feature, like tongue-and-groove panelling. Play with variations on straight lines, using panelling vertically or horizontally, or employing timber slats with gaps.

If there are particularly dominant, one-off architectural features, such as steel pillars within an open-plan space or a decorative arch, build these into your vision. Think through any practical implications: if a column, for example, is awkwardly placed, how can you get the best possible use out of the divided space? Consider the aesthetic impact: will you stick to understated joinery and plain walls so that the eye is drawn to these imposing elements?

If, by contrast, there is zero architectural detailing, choose one or two new features that can be repeated throughout to inject character. Varied window styles might be replaced with smart Crittall steel/metal-framed versions, or pick a distinctive pattern of limestone to be made up into fireplaces, bathroom splashbacks and kitchen worktops. If there is limited or no budget to replace architectural features, then think laterally. Something as simple as painting non-identical styles of door or window frame all in one deep colour can impart cohesion. Ultimately, you are aiming for a tightly coordinated, architecturally uniform look.

So iron out stylistic irregularities, be consistent in your detailing and spend money on good-quality materials and essential building work if necessary. Once in place, you can respond to architectural bones in a variety of ways. A 19th-century house with period features can be painted in strong colours and take on a very modern aesthetic. Alternatively, a new-build property with sleek surfaces can reflect a cosy vibe, with the addition of carefully selected tactile textiles. Get the bones right, and they will become a springboard for fresh thoughts and brilliant ideas.

# THINK ...SIZE & SHAPE

EXPERT THINKING

“It is important that each room continues seamlessly into the next. Use the same colour paint and wooden floors to link, mixing vintage and modern to add personality.”

**MELANIE IRELAND**
*DESIGNER/OWNER*

**THIS PAGE** Emphasize a dramatic high ceiling with custom-built joinery. These shelves also make good use of otherwise redundant space.

**OPPOSITE LEFT** Rooms with very high ceilings can lack intimacy. This pendant light fills empty space and adds character.

**OPPOSITE RIGHT** Use a dominant feature, such as a vertical support, to divide up a space into separate living zones.

It is human nature to wish for plenty of space at home. We think extra rooms and bigger proportions are the Holy Grail, and many of us rush into knocking down walls in pursuit of the ultimate expanse. But stop and think again. Yes, large rooms create brilliant social spaces and are great for young families needing to multi-task. But what you gain in living space, you lose in intimacy. Smaller rooms afford privacy, are easier to decorate and offer a more versatile mix of accommodation.

You can't begin to maximize potential at home until you've mused over size and shape. First, contemplate the bigger picture by walking from room to room and creating a mind map. Find a piece of paper, write 'big room' or 'sloping ceilings' in the middle, then jot down your initial thoughts, both positive and negative, in a circle around those words. There's nothing like tapping into immediate reactions to get to the crux of your requirements. If every room is large, you'll quickly realize the need to coax out quiet corners and imbue warming ambience, while retaining the dramatic proportions. A tiny flat will prompt notes on creating spaces that flow together, using colour or matching surfaces to bind them.

Consider, too, the balance of size and shape between rooms. In an ideal world, at least one active zone like the kitchen, sitting room or hall should be located in the biggest room(s); even if there is just one larger space, it gives everyone 'room to breathe', visually and physically. Moving between airy living zones and tiny rooms alters mood and creates an interesting daily dynamic. Work mindfully to play up those contrasts of size and shape; colour, scale of furniture and pattern are powerful tools to help you do it.

TOM FORD
EL ATLAS DE NUESTRO TIEMPO
THE TIMES ATLAS OF THE WORLD

Big rooms are a cause for celebration. Don't be intimidated by vast expanses of wall or high ceilings: flaunt them. Custom-built shelves and cabinets should be confidently taken right up to the ceiling; too low, and the proportions will look mean and skimpy. (It doesn't matter if you can't reach every single book – use a library ladder.) Giant pendant lights, perhaps in dramatic or sculptural shapes, are brilliant for showing off lofty ceilings, and while you're at it, scale up art.

Keep an eye on furniture size and quantities; don't overstuff the room just because you can. Often, generously proportioned rooms look best when they are quite sparsely furnished. Balance a tall room with a long refectory table, a pair of matching sofas or L-shaped modular seating. Many companies will custom-make pieces to generous sizes for remarkably little extra cost.

Most designers love the challenge of designing small rooms, and so should you. If any negative thoughts come to mind, such as lack of light or scant space for furniture, sweep them away. The secret is to design a compact space exactly as you would a normal-size room, then scale up, not down. Choose large motifs rather than tiny patterns, two armchairs rather than one, rich, dark paint shades rather than light ones. The more confident the decoration, the stronger an identity your small room will have, and the less everyone will notice the petite proportions. It helps to think about these tiny spaces in a task-specific way – will the room be a study, a breakfast room or a grown-up sitting room? Then joinery and furniture can be tailored, and possessions edited to fit in.

As for irregularly shaped rooms, consider how the available space can best be used, and forget about traditional room labels such as 'bedroom'. Sloping attic walls can prompt ideas for creative play spaces for kids, who won't care about head height. A high-ceilinged, narrow room might become an atmospheric bathroom, while a slim length of corridor can be turned into a hot-desking work area. Take heart: the quirkier the original space, the harder you will have to think but the more inventive the solution will be.

**OPPOSITE** This modestly proportioned sitting room has been well filled, but the tightly coordinated colour scheme ensures a chic and uncluttered look.

**ABOVE** Expert planning pays dividends in a small space. This bay window is fitted with a built-in banquette, a breakfast table and stools that can be tucked beneath.

ACADEMIA

# THINK ...BUDGET & RESOURCES

EXPERT THINKING

“If you create a room around one expensive piece, like any beautiful thing it will have lots of character. Balance it with less costly items, simple in design or texture.”

**MICHELA IMPERIALI KLEMOS**
*INTERIOR DESIGNER*

**LEFT** Operate budget on a sliding scale, both financial and visual. If you've blown everything on a beautiful piece of marble for a kitchen island, painted cabinets are a smart budget choice.

**BELOW** Inexpensive paper lanterns, used creatively, make a brilliant choice for a family space. Early clever thinking when planning electric wiring makes multiple hangings possible.

Everyone has a budget, so don't be shy to confront finances head on. Whether you have a vast or a tiny sum, think of it in glowing, positive terms, as this money is your gateway to a chic, pulled-together home. Work out exactly how much you have to spend and how much extra might be borrowed, such as a home loan or adding to the mortgage, and allocate 10% for unforeseen problems. Write out a one-, three- and five-year plan to see how larger costs, such as buying new furniture, might be spread.

Think of your budget not as a constraint but as a balancing process. Creative balancing means understanding your ultimate decorative goal and what quality or financial sacrifices you're prepared to make. What were your decorative priorities as jotted on your mind maps? The first priority should always be to get the shell right, as it is costly to make alterations later. Investing in a good architect may seem expensive, but will save vital money and time. Upgrading plumbing or rewiring makes a disappointing dent in the budget, but the investment endures for years. And if you're wavering over justifying the cost of cast-iron radiators or a new oak floor, remember you will touch these quality basics every single day. Save money instead with brand-free paints or do the decorating yourself.

If you have a very tight budget and there can be no major structural alterations, luxury is still possible. Use quality materials or splurge buys sparingly but in show-off places. A marble splashback in the bathroom, a panel of antique mirror above a fireplace or a mid-20th-century light fitting in the hall sets the quality bar high, and draws the eye from cut-price additions elsewhere. Once you adopt a positive mindset towards adding luxury in creative little bursts balanced with money-saving options, the process becomes addictive.

Before spending a penny, consider existing home features that can be revamped. A wood fireplace, for example, gets a smart new look if repainted in a colour, while kitchen cabinets can be refaced with custom-made high-gloss doors. Make this evaluation process a careful edit, rather than a rapid cut-and-paste job. Then shop around for materials as far in advance as possible. The luxury of time means you can surf the net for end-of-line bargains or plan visits to out-of-town warehouses, where costs may be lower. You might return to an architectural salvage yard several times on a slow but ultimately fruitful hunt for teak internal doors.

The more time you can devote to mulling over varying decorative options, the greater the creative scope. It gives you breathing space to consider customizing, which can save money. Customizing does require an element of bravery, a 'what if?' attitude, but thinking outside the box is fun. Budget storage units from a chain store can be spray-painted in high gloss and wall-hung in multiples for an elegant new look. Or buy up a bargain patchwork of mixed, reclaimed encaustic tiles to create a unique bathroom floor.

Allow a 'finishing off' budget. There is nothing more frustrating than waving goodbye to the builders, only to ruin your new home with shabby possessions. Try to keep aside 10% of the entire budget for fresh soft furnishings or a stand-out piece or two of furniture (or spend your 'emergencies' fund at the end of the project). And if all the money has gone, inexpensive but cool chain-store accessories can be lifesavers.

**BELOW** Every home needs a wow factor, so work out your own. A piece of contemporary art can successfully dominate a room, with no need for expensive decoration elsewhere.

# 2 THINK LIFESTYLE

05.05.03

# THINK ...FAMILY ZONES

EXPERT THINKING

"Every family needs plenty of storage! Make the kitchen as freestanding as possible. Ergonomics and practicality matter, but also try contrasting finishes on worktops in different areas for interest and texture."

**CATHERINE SMITH**
*INTERIOR DESIGNER*

**OPPOSITE** Choose robust surfaces, from a wooden tabletop to a loam floor, but don't forget a cosy vibe; sheepskins work well.

**ABOVE LEFT** Add accessories that play a part in family living. Lighting candles heralds the shift from school time to homecoming.

**ABOVE RIGHT** Open storage reflects a casual lifestyle, but plan enough shelves to hold all the everyday essentials.

The process of thinking through how your home will ultimately be used is the first step towards hard-working, beautiful rooms. Careful consideration will reveal what each space must deliver, and how you want it to look. Start by examining your lifestyle.

The most successful family zones will work perfectly for weekdays and weekends, adults and kids, one person or ten, in daylight and by night. They will also allow space for movement, generate fun and visual stimulation, and be brilliant at multi-tasking. That's the theory, anyway – now think about your own ideal family space. Brainstorm with the kids, jotting down adjectives that sum up the perfect space. Words such as 'busy' and 'happy' will be key. Repeat the same process with emotions or colours, and alongside 'chilled out' and 'joyful' you might focus on colour choices like 'scarlet', 'tangerine' and 'lipstick pink'. These are early pointers towards an appropriate decorating style.

Now approach the upcoming design from a task- and people-specific angle. What activities will take place in the family zone? Those with small children will require space to play, a spot for easy meals and quiet TV watching. Criteria change again for older kids and teens as activities expand to studying, gaming, watching films, cooking and general hanging out, not to mention adults' requirements. Who will share this zone (friends, pets) and with what other items (bikes, footballs, musical instruments)? The more information you have to hand, the better at multi-tasking this room will be.

Ponder how your family area is currently used, whether for parties, book-group gatherings or homework. Watch how everyone in your household 'settles' each night and on weekends. Where do they congregate or disperse to, why and at what time? If everyone

**ABOVE** Scrutinize the casual 'treasures' that ebb and flow in a family living area and weave these into the decorative mix. A display of 'found' objects feels authentic.

**RIGHT** A fireplace or wood-burning stove creates a second, equally important, place to gather away from the kitchen table. A low-slung leather armchair or a rocking chair are brilliant extras.

is disappearing off to their bedrooms or to the study, then reconfiguring the room into a stimulating shared space can rewire the way a family connects.

Finding the right location matters. Think of the family zone as the nucleus or nerve centre, the hub. It doesn't matter what word you use, but it's a good way to remember that this zone must be truly accessible. Can there be more than one exit/entry point, or access to outdoor space or an interconnecting room so that everyone is drawn here easily? Designing a family zone around the kitchen makes sense, as food is a natural magnet. Sometimes families create a 'chill-out room', but such spaces may end up as unused satellite rooms if they are not en route to somewhere more interesting.

Any new structural additions should be robust enough to withstand 24/7 use, yet streamlined to maximize every centimetre of space. In a family zone, storage is priority number one. Devising sturdy, good-looking storage at the planning stage means that it will be integrated into the fabric of the room. Go for bold choices: full-height, deep cupboards, chunky shelves, built-in window seating with storage space beneath. Follow through the scaled-up theme with kitchen appliances and hardware: a range-style cooker, super-size refrigerator, cast-iron radiators and easy-grab doorknobs. If you choose such features early on and then plan other decorative fittings around them, they will still work well even in a small space.

*** THINK AHEAD ...**
**and be experimental. Each new decorating project requires a brilliant fresh scheme, so don't cling to a familiar palette.**

**LEFT** The best-planned family living space works hard for both kids and adults. It should feel inspirational across the generations, too. Tread a fine line between picking vivid colour accents that will appeal to all and using them in a sophisticated and practical way. In this open-plan sitting room, bright lacquered 'boxes' add visual zip to the shelves, but they are hollow, thus providing an extra layer of storage.

**OPPOSITE** Give due thought to how a space will look (and feel) at all stages of the day and night. Textured charcoal walls look cool and, teamed with accents of bright aqua and blue, don't overpower by day. In the evening, paired with low lighting, they are instrumental in creating a warm, intimate family area for socializing or TV watching.

Family zones endure constant wear and tear. Rather than trying to fight this, mull over decorative surfaces that will go with the flow. Lived-in surfaces and fabrics add to a laid-back mood and look amazing. If you're not so keen on a distressed look, investigate easy-care materials that won't mark. For upholstery, try fabrics designed for outdoor furniture (as these will be splash-proof), or use big-print cottons or geometric-patterned weaves.

Go back to your initial word jottings when you choose furniture. If the list included 'comfy' or 'sharing', invest in expansive pieces: a long dining table or a sociable circular pedestal style, a bench and retro dining chairs and a deep, cosy sofa. Ultimately, devising a family zone is all about flexibility. By its nature, family life is constantly evolving and adapting, so actively reflect that fluid lifestyle in the furnishings that you choose.

MAGRITTE

# THINK ...SOCIABLE SPACES

EXPERT THINKING

"Go for generous scale, ensure sofas and armchairs are similar heights, positioned to allow cross-conversations. Robust materials make guests feel at home; if a drink gets knocked over, it doesn't matter."

**EMMA OLDHAM**
*INTERIOR DESIGNER*

**OPPOSITE AND ABOVE** For a large room to really gel, both decoratively and practically, there must be a palpable sense of intimacy. In this multipurpose sitting room, the deliberate mix of ceiling heights contributes to that cosy feeling, as does the muted wall colour and the dense, rich mix of textures and patterns. Rugs can become really useful tools to mark out separate zones. Here, the patterned one provides a central focus for the main seating area, while the animal hide, set to one side, delineates a second space complete with a daybed.

We may all have varying definitions of sociable spaces, but a good start is to think of them as modern-day drawing rooms with attitude; beautiful and expertly planned, yet packed with ambience and a dash of drama. Such rooms are also the 'public' face of your home, for entertaining friends. But that doesn't mean you must design them in a formal manner. Instead, look through a lifestyle lens. By focusing on how you like to entertain, you'll gain insight into creative decorative solutions.

Start by considering the way you socialize. Do you prefer large or small gatherings, daytime or evening entertaining, dinners or drinks? If you're a party animal, consider bold furnishings that generate a sense of theatre. Is intimacy the focus? That's the cue for furniture in clubby clusters, ambient lighting and cocooning textures. Now reverse your thinking. Think of friends' homes, or bars and restaurants where you've enjoyed a laid-back evening. Pinpoint how the decoration enhanced the mood. What elements made you feel especially relaxed?

Back in your own home, take a few moments to imagine your ideal party. Picture friends entering your sociable space. Where are they going to stand:

by the fire, around a sofa, by doors to the garden? Is there capacity for sitting in separate conversational groups? Where will drinks and food go? Visualizing like this helps enormously when planning layout. Everyday seating arrangements may not work for larger groups, but too many extra chairs may result in an awkward 'waiting room' look. Plan layout in zoned sections. Even in a small room, aim for one central seating area – perhaps twin sofas opposite one another – plus portable side chairs to form a satellite conversation zone, and an ottoman for a cosy third spot.

Imagining how your sociable spaces are going to work means thinking like a stage manager. With seating planned, what will be your most useful

**THIS PAGE** Pick multipurpose pieces that can work together or alone. Think hard about marrying form and function; side tables must be practical, but chosen mindfully they will deliver a dynamic visual punch, too.

**OPPOSITE** The greater the mix of lighting, the more versatile the room. This open-plan sitting room can be a soulful space or a party spot, with its combination of task lights clamped to shelves, mid-level standard and table lamps, plus a low-slung pendant over the dining table.

(and decorative) props? Side tables are often an afterthought, but in reality are multifunctional and inject visual interest. Nests of tables are brilliant for small spaces yet spring into action for parties, a narrow console can masquerade as a sideboard and low-level tables work as stools. Lighting is a great tool. A pendant light hanging low over twin armchairs or a floor-standing lamp near a sofa will pool ambient light and encourage conversation clusters.

This is also your show-off space, imbued with your personality, and it tells the story of who you are. Accessorize your room with possessions that you love and pieces that deliver the image you want to present to the world. Visitors will appreciate a carefully considered juxtaposition of attractive objects or well-chosen art. Showcase a ceramics collection that can spark a conversation, or an exotic find for which you have an anecdote to tell. Accessories don't

**THIS PAGE** If space allows, go both maxi and mini with a large formal seating area and a smaller, more relaxed cluster of stools and/or armchairs tucked to one side. This arrangement works best if the furniture silhouettes are kept low, promoting easy commication.

need to be expensive, but they do need to add glamour, interest or, at the very least, a beautiful sculptural silhouette.

Sociable spaces must work both for everyday and also for parties. So picking fabrics is a challenge: too smart and they are not practical, too plain and there's no sense of drama. Return to those early thoughts about entertaining preferences. Do you want the room to glide from coffee mornings to full-on glitz? Then plan fabrics to work in layers. Upholster sofas in plain linens or wool. Add an occasional chair in a punchy geometric weave or a pouffe in silver leather. When it's party time, put the colourful pieces centre stage and replace everyday cushions with sequinned or velvet styles.

5
FLASH
GORDON

# THINK ...QUIET RETREATS

**EXPERT THINKING**

"Everyone needs his/her own little space, but it's preferable if every space is connected, too. Keep things classic, then change the interior with small details like coloured cushions or lampshades."

**CAROLINE VAN THILLO**
*INTERIOR DESIGNER*

**THIS PAGE** No physical barriers keep this area private and yet, equipped with its rug, lighting and art, it creates a successful illusion of peace and quiet.

**OPPOSITE** A daybed fits neatly into a spare corner and is dual-purpose: it allows space to stretch out solo, or can be shared, bench-style, by several people.

Every home should offer its occupants the chance for a quiet retreat. Carving out a peaceful spot in modern homes isn't always easy, though, with the popularity of open-plan spaces, mezzanine levels or interconnected rooms. For sure, we can all escape into a study or bedroom. But the ideal compromise is to plan for quiet corners that sit within the main living space. For parents, this can offer a clever bit of reverse psychology: if you remain on view, rather than behind a door, kids won't pester you. And for all of us, the ability to relax quietly within the home hub is simply more sociable.

Focus first on function. How best can this micro retreat serve you? You will most likely be reading, working (or film watching) on a laptop or tablet, or talking on the phone. Work out all the services needed: an excellent source of light, a power point, warmth, no draughts. Practical furniture basics will include a comfortable yet supportive chair, a bookcase or low table, preferably with at least one drawer, and a wall-mounted or floor-standing task lamp or perfectly positioned pendant light. There needs to be sufficient space in the quiet corner for everything to remain in situ 24/7 so that you can just flop down and use it.

Walk around your home with inquisitive eyes and think about which unused corners are going to work best. Sometimes we're so familiar with our home environment that we cease to 'see' its potential. Having to re-evaluate existing space to fulfil a new, specific task can be a refreshing exercise. Certain areas always work well: a portion of a long hallway, the end of a wide landing or the turn on a stair, a corner of a large sitting room, the 'dead' space beneath a sloping roof. A desk can be tucked into the area beneath a staircase, or built into a fireplace alcove.

Will there be the budget and the square footage to add a physical division to improve privacy? One end of a long living room, for example, might be sectioned off with floor-to-ceiling glazed metal doors, which let in light and views but deaden noise. Including an internal 'window' within a section of wall is a similar but space-saving alternative, or you could install full-height sliding doors. Pushing these just a third of the way across, rather than shutting off the space completely, can be all it takes to induce calm. In a period cottage, a heavy linen curtain hung from a ceiling-mounted pole can screen off a peaceful area. If physical divisions are not possible, use trompe l'oeil decorative tricks. Placing an armchair on a circular rug will visually 'separate' a quiet zone, while a panel of graphic wallpaper can define a desk zone and make a strong decorative statement.

Whether glimpsed or on full view, a peaceful retreat needs to look good. Creating these little solo spots is a more exacting discipline than designing an equipment-jammed home office with a door that shuts. There are choices here. Either design a quiet retreat to dovetail visually with the rest of the room, decorating with coordinating textures and colours, or use it as a show-off space. Adding a design-conscious chair makes an instant impact. Select an armchair, recliner or swivel chair with a curvaceous silhouette, such as a mid-20th-century classic like Arne Jacobsen's Swan chair. Or, to create drama in a room with a subtle, neutral colour scheme, choose lupin blue or vibrant scarlet upholstery, or a bold patterned fabric. Have fun with dramatic looks, but also ensure the chair provides support, is comfortable and that you can recline or curl up in it.

A quiet zone doesn't have to be a solo space. In a family house, consider creating a peaceful corner with twin armchairs or a loveseat, making it the ideal spot for private conversation. Increasingly, furniture companies are designing chic, diminutive sofas perfect for space-compromised homes; these make great choices. Or invest in one or two chunky-knit pouffes, a chic new take on the casual beanbag, which can be transported to a tranquil corner by the kids.

For some, a quiet desk area is essential; one step removed from the bustle of the kitchen table, yet still part of the public domain. Let that need inform your furniture choices. Of course, a desk must be functional, but it should also look smart. Many furniture companies now offer modern takes on mid-20th-century styling: desks with neat proportions, slender legs and perhaps a flash of coloured worktop. These styles sit perfectly within an elegant living space. Look for a design with a few drawers so that work paraphernalia can be tucked away, or site it next to a bookcase, where files can be hidden in wicker baskets. Accessories must fuse aesthetically with room decor. So instead of a metal task lamp, pick a cool table lamp with a sculptural metal or blown-glass base, and rather than an 'office' chair, add a trendy swivel design.

**ABOVE AND OPPOSITE** There is a fine line between creating a quiet nook and keeping it linked with everyday living areas. This desk is tucked into a purpose-built study corner, yet the mirror acts as a connection with the rest of the space. Identical joinery detailing, and shared wallpaper and flooring, also helps cohesion.

*** THINK TWICE ... about forgotten corners. Wrap a custom-built bookshelf along a wall, dovetail it into the corner and keep on going.**

CHARLIE'S
INBOX

**THIS PAGE AND OPPOSITE** A large or L-shaped room may present the chance to steal space for a separate quiet spot at one end. If possible, place the desk close to a window, or hang a soulful painting above it, for a contemplative view.

**★ THINK BIG ... and contrast carefully chosen scaled-up accessories with a simple setting.**

pirelli calendars

# 3 THINK INSPIRED

# THINK ...COLOUR

EXPERT THINKING

"If you're afraid of colour, just one wall can easily be redone, or play with coloured accessories. There are no rules when designing a home, no colours that are better than others, no stupid ideas."

**ANNE GEISTDOERFER**

*INTERIOR DESIGNER/ARCHITECT*

We all know that colour at home provokes an emotional response. Whether soothing or stimulating, deep or pale, we can't help but react to it. Colour also influences our visitors and the ambience in our environment; it even affects the look of our furniture. It can feel like a huge responsibility to pick exactly the 'right' shades. Instead, try adopting an alternative mindset. Focus on your own personality and this will help you take back control. Are you peaceful? Active? Cheerful? What shades enhance your natural characteristics? And where do these definitions point to in colour terms: 'soulful' may dictate a moody indigo; 'lively' can suggest warm lilac. Rather than passively waiting to be influenced by colours, pick tones that specifically chime with your personality.

So far, so good, but it can be scary to commit to colour, especially over large expanses. Using neutrals often feels safer. But you'd never choose to dress from head to toe in taupe, so why do so at home? Face your fears; remember that walls can be painted over, and that it is good to be pushed out of the comfort zone. Feel positive about embracing new shades. Using a bold choice that's in tune with your personality not only feels comfortable but also imparts authority, looks grown up and tells the world that you've made an informed decision. Committing to a colour is a deeply personal way of stamping a decorative statement at home.

Hone initial colour ideas by experimenting. Forget about trawling DIY stores for sample paint pots. Instead, get watercolour paints, paper and a brush, then paint the key tones you see outside the window, whether they are the spring greens of a field or the steel grey of an urban landscape. Does this provoke fresh ideas to try? Open your wardrobe: what shades do you wear? Could they form the basis of a scheme? Examine high fashion and hip interiors shops with a conscious 'colour' eye. What is new in the 'ether'? This exercise is not about following fashion. It's about nudging yourself out of a colour rut and adding unusual influences, from chartreuse to vivid teal, to kickstart an imaginative palette.

Instead of thinking in terms of pale or dark, focus on the level of colour saturation. It's time to move on from white and the safety of knocked-back neutrals. The newest way to use colour is to indulge in dense, glowing shades. Strong pewter, chalky denim or deep cappuccino will all look sharp and make a room feel tailored, while jewel shades like amethyst create cosy evening rooms.

**OPPOSITE** If walls are in a bright shade, stick to monochrome, muted or patterned accessories and art so that they don't 'fight' with the colour.

**THIS PAGE** Furniture finishes must be included in the equation. Here, a black table, rather than pale timber, provides a robust balance against the strong yellow.

SCHILDERKUNST
VAN A TOT Z
DE WARE DE WEVER
MENSEN
KINSHASA CONGO
UPDATE

**OPPOSITE** Linking colour from room to room is a brilliant way to create a sense of visual unity, but apply it to different surfaces. Experiment with a dark shade for custom-built cabinetry, then use it on walls and blinds or curtains in the adjoining space.

**RIGHT** A black wall looks super-chic. But it will also draw attention directly towards paintings and photos, so take time to think through choices.

If you're brave enough, take the colour right across all the walls and joinery. For a gentler effect, use softer saturated shades such as aubergine/eggplant or navy on floors or ceilings.

It's a good idea to choose a tightly edited palette, with just three or four shades that can be reinterpreted in varying combinations throughout your home. Do this at the start, rather than selecting colours on an ad hoc basis, so that even if you decorate room by room over time you still have your original plan to refer back to. Having a master colour palette makes sense. It means you can play with balance. It's overpowering to use dark shades right through a home and equally boring to have pale tones everywhere. Engineer a visual dynamic by having some moody and some airy rooms. Think about using colour 'threads'. Pick one vibrant shade – for example scarlet, ochre or turquoise – and repeat splashes of that colour in every single room. But vary the amount, with an entire wall of colour in one room and just a curtain binding in another. Colour threads will pull together an interior into one neat, visual package.

As well as energizing entire surfaces such as walls, certain colours can be used as a contouring tool. Useful shades are charcoal, plum, black or ink. Such tones look punchy used on custom-built joinery and can highlight and elongate doors or windows, as well as drawing attention to pretty mouldings. They can also be used to impart architectural interest where little exists. Fine black lines painted onto walls, for example, give a trompe l'oeil panelled effect. Dark woodwork balances bright wall colours effectively, whereas bright white can create too harsh a contrast.

Whatever colours you choose, remember that clever combining means mixing, not matching. If you've chosen to upholster key pieces of furniture in two or three brights, introduce the odd pastel or sludgy shade, too. It can be fun to add 'off' hues to the master palette, just to shake things up a bit. Think of coloured accessories as the jewellery of the room. Arm yourself with a pool of extras, from vases to cushions; dip into that collection regularly, and you can refresh not just the surroundings but also your eye.

**THIS PAGE AND OPPOSITE** When using a deep colour on walls, pick out similar (but not matching) tones to echo around the room. To get the most natural balance, use these tones in varying quantities, from a hint in a piece of artwork, to a larger block of colour on a cushion.

RICHARD PRINCE
INSPIRATION
the iconic house
GARDENING
ANDREW MARTIN INTERIOR DESIGN REVIEW
VOGUE LIVING HOUSES, GARDENS, PEOPLE

# THINK ...TEXTURE

EXPERT THINKING

"Painted floorboards reflect light, making a space feel bigger. Natural plaster and polished concrete have a soft patina. The finish adds depth and atmosphere to any home, ancient or modern."

**NICOLA HARDING**
*INTERIOR DESIGNER*

AMOUR
PARIS

**OPPOSITE** Compose varying textures in a room like a painting, aiming for a pleasing balance of finish, colour and pattern. This room successfully mixes moderate quantities of dominant cowhide with a subtle concrete floor, matt wooden shelves with the quiet sheen of a metal fireplace and the mellow colours of wood with bright lacquered paint.

**ABOVE AND RIGHT** Planning and installing a matching floor, splashback and worksurface gives a particularly smart, considered finish. In this family kitchen, the polished loam used for all three has a soft black tone and will gently 'distress' over time. For a seamless look, choose a range cooker and sink in muted colours to match.

There is more to texture than meets the eye – quite literally. Textured surfaces are the new stars of design; increasingly, interior designers are making visually arresting surfaces the centre point of a decorative scheme. So think of texture as a fully integrated element in the decorating process and, alongside your master colour palette, compile a texture storyboard, too.

First, think practical. Hard surfaces, from worksurfaces to floors, must be durable. Make that a given, then decide between textures that will age well, or robust surfaces guaranteed to retain their crisp good looks. For a patina that weathers well, go for wooden or engineered floorboards, for limestone, terracotta or sandstone in reclaimed, tumbled or versions or for leather.

*** THINK BACK ...**
**to why you love your home. Honour its historical roots, modernize for the future, then enjoy living in the present.**

**OPPOSITE** A flash of brass feels elegant yet modern, but use it sparingly for a clean, crisp look. A specialist metal supplier will cut to fit; use metal on an island unit, as a splashback or to panel a section of wall.

**THIS PAGE** It is fun to play with expectations. This simple bleached timber cladding is given a surprise decorative finish with the use of curved and feminine door fronts.

**THIS PAGE** Just because tiles are square doesn't mean you need to use them in regular blocks. It is more imaginative to experiment and vary the horizontal line of a splashback, or take the tiles across a worksurface and along the front of a unit.

**BELOW** For a large tiled expanse, look beyond plain colours and investigate hand-glazed clay tiles with pearlized, iridescent or metallic finishes, or those with subtle colour gradations. Used en masse, this adds depth to the finish.

**RIGHT** A trompe l'oeil textured paint effect needn't be restricted to a plain plastered wall. Take it right the way across custom-built cupboards, too, for a smart, unified look.

*** THINK TWICE ...**

**before replacing nondescript doors. Gloss-paint them in a strong muted shade and add tactile, shapely handles.**

Surfaces that always look pristine include porcelain and ceramic tiles, poured resin floors and polished concrete. Ask yourself: is this textured surface fit for purpose? Will it work hard for my lifestyle?

Next, mull over visual appeal. If you source an unusual textured surface at the start, be brave enough to make it the central focus. This is where the fun starts, because there is now a glorious choice of extravagantly patterned materials and innovative new combinations of classic finishes. Consider veined marble, onyx or rose quartz, veneers such as walnut or bird's eye maple, or high-fashion mixes from limestone with copper inlay to marble inset with mother-of-pearl. Abstract visual effects include 3-D concrete wall tiles or toughened glass wall panels with metallic paint. Think about colour: pale blue marble, or limestone in honey, black or pink tones. Are there defined motifs within your chosen texture that can be echoed within a patterned fabric or the shape of a piece of furniture?

Consider the tactile factor. At home we touch worksurfaces, handles and walls constantly, and, even if it's just subliminal, texture can either soothe or annoy us. You need to satisfy your eye, your fingertips – and the soles of your feet. For organic, nubbly finishes, pick natural wallcoverings like cork, jute or woven paper, or coconut or timber panelling. Satisfying flooring choices might include rugged travertine blocks, reclaimed French terracotta tiles or embossed leather. How will these finishes look translated onto a large or a small scale? A detailed choice like iridescent abalone shell or mother-of-pearl tiles looks best used in small spaces – as a splashback, perhaps. For large expanses, choose something abstract like satin aluminium tiles.

Consider how your carefully edited textures will work together. If you want to make a strong decorative statement with a particular surface, be confident and employ large quantities. A wonderfully patterned wood veneer can be used to clad walls, cupboard doors and even internal doors. In a bathroom, take brightly coloured glass mosaics up the walls and across the floor. For an equally powerful look, choose contrasting textures such as glossy ceramic tiles, a polished plaster wall finish and a resin floor, but all in the same colour. Using textured finishes in such a manner is a great way to deflect attention away from a room lacking in architectural features, or to disguise irregularities such as bumpy plastered walls or an unattractive low ceiling.

**LEFT** If your budget doesn't permit luxurious and exotic stone surfaces, instead look for a coffee table or a console sporting an eye-catching stone tabletop.

**OPPOSITE** Used across a large expanse, this rosewood panelling ceases to be just a texture and becomes part of the colour scheme. To balance rich tones, look to warm, natural shades, such as tomato, indigo and ochre.

Another option is to play around with conventional textures. Confound expectations by using an inexpensive basic, such as plain subway-style tiles, and fixing them on the vertical, rather than horizontally. Take materials out of context. Tiles, for example, are usually restricted to wet rooms, so instead of putting patterned cement tiles in a shower, see how dynamic they look on one wall in a home study. Try unexpected juxtapositions, from a splashback of vivid green malachite teamed with a stainless-steel washbasin, to a sliver of copper worktop adjacent to white laminate kitchen units. Even a simple change, like using black or coloured grout with tiles, imparts a new slant to plain basics.

Textured materials require careful planning from the start, and may need a specialist to install them. They may also need to be professionally sealed to retain their good looks. So using texture is not a cheap option, but weaving in just a small quantity of a tactile material will deliver an imaginative vibe at home. Think of your home as a jigsaw, then choose woven, matt or glossy textures to spice up the final picture.

# THINK ...PATTERN

EXPERT THINKING

"Be brave and use pattern on all walls. Feature walls lack the courage of conviction. Large repeats look better in rooms with high ceilings; choose busier designs for smaller spaces."

**BUNNY TURNER**
*INTERIOR DESIGNER*

*** THINK BIG ...**

**clash abstract wallpaper with a contrast pattern floor, but paint skirtings, doors and cornices in a single bright shade to link.**

**THIS PAGE** Forget about coordinating cushions. Mixing up unexpected motifs, linked with common colourways, is a brilliant way to modernize a plain sofa. It's also a start for building up confidence when using pattern.

**OPPOSITE** Many of the new geometric wallpapers combine a nod to our retro past with on-trend colours. They are an inspired choice for family spaces, so accessorize them with a relaxed, tongue-in-cheek approach.

Now we've emerged from over a decade of plains, embracing pattern again feels new. Leave classic florals to one side for once. Graphic motifs, including circles, squares, chevrons and diagonals, are more exciting and surprisingly versatile. Delving into abstracts delivers a tailored, grown-up look or, when combined with acid or bold colour, gives a funky spin. Such patterns need a little considered planning and expert balancing to look their best. The reward is a chic room with a strong personality.

Many of us shy away from pattern because large expanses can seem overwhelming. But paintings, bookshelves and curtains are all mitigating factors that dilute the impact. Pattern on floors will be broken up with pieces of furniture,

**OPPOSITE** Tune into how a particular pattern makes you feel. Small-scale geometrics look sharp, broad stripes are breezy and Moroccan-inspired designs are pretty in a bedroom.

**LEFT** Look beyond the obvious sources, such as wallpapers, fabrics and rugs, and start to see patterns in less-expected places, from a rattan stool to the weave of a plain fabric.

and anyway, we don't walk around with our eyes cast down. Hold your nerve and realize that pattern is an ally. Visit showrooms to see fabrics and wallpapers in large expanses, and check out large, small and mid-range designs.

Scaled-up pattern on walls tricks the eye and makes a room feel bigger. Remember that contrasting motifs, in varying quantities throughout your home, will usefully alter the mood from one room to the next. When choosing wallpaper, consider all potential colourways, as monochrome or bold colour versions appear radically different. Muted colours may seem 'safe', but when used from floor to ceiling the pattern may recede. If you've opted for a dramatic motif, don't feel constrained to use only plain furnishings. A more balanced and richly visual effect is achieved by combining a medium-scale patterned rug, subtle textural weaves for upholstery and contrast prints on cushions. Muted or dark paintwork also balances the impact. For a sophisticated finish, keep to monochromes or use a maximum of three colours. A very cool alternative is to keep walls plain, with decorative wallpaper on the ceiling.

It is a timely moment to choose an abstract rug, as there are designer and chainstore versions aplenty. Many can be commissioned in custom sizes or colours, and specialist rug companies may let you try them out first at home. Pattern underfoot is the equivalent of a decorative coat lining: it offers a visual fillip each time you look down. Patterned rugs are useful tools when it comes to zoning spaces. In a hall, a decorative runner or stair carpet naturally directs the eye towards entertaining spaces. And in an open-plan area, pick rugs in similar shades but with motifs on a sliding scale, to vary the dynamic. A graphic rug featuring tiny spots works well in a peaceful sitting area, then ramp up the mood with giant multicoloured dots in the play zone.

Think carefully about where pattern stops and starts and aim for a gentle overlapping of contrasting motifs. In a kitchen with high-gloss lacquered units and a squiggle-tiled floor, tile the island unit up to skirting height, blurring horizontal and vertical boundaries. If you have curtains with broad horizontal bands, team them with armchairs upholstered in narrower stripes. And for soft furnishing options, play around with convention. You don't have to use patterned fabric en masse. Instead, highlight a bold motif by using a section of it as a central panel on a sofa or on the back of a dining chair.

# THINK ...KITCHENS

EXPERT THINKING

"Kitchens should be at the heart of the home. Include a large, user-friendly table, or, in a small interior, make the kitchen open out into the sitting room. Colour embeds strength and personality."

**SARAH LAVOINE**
*INTERIOR DESIGNER*

S M E

The kitchen has become the soul centre of the home. We expect it to be welcoming, comfortable and decorative, forgetting that it remains the most hard-working room. When it comes to planning, of course it is tempting to kick off by examining tear sheets of gorgeous examples. But instead be clear-headed and ask yourself who, what and how? Who is this kitchen for: solo use, couples, family? What activities will take place here: is it an indulgent foodie's kitchen or a grab-and-go meal station? And finally, how flexible is your budget?

First, think practical. Start with appliances and sinks, because these are daily workhorses. Efficient equipment should make routine tasks easier (and more pleasurable), so invest in the best you can afford. If your star buys are identified early, you'll get the appliances you want now, they will arrive in good time and there's leeway to reduce costs on decorative finishes later on. It's also easier to tailor kitchen cabinets around appliance dimensions. Every kitchen should be planned around the classic work triangle – cold food storage, cooking area and dishwashing zone – so mull over practicalities in that order. And while you're at it, you can match appliances to your lifestyle.

**LEFT AND OPPOSITE** With careful planning, an inexpensive kitchen can look chic. This one blends clever ideas like plain handle-free doors added to budget cabinets, plus the inspired choice of chair upholstery matched to the refrigerator.

**ABOVE** Open shelving looks smart when equipped with beautiful vintage containers.

For a family or cook's kitchen, curvy retro or American-style refrigerators offer plenty of storage. They look as good tucked next to a run of built-in units as standing solo like a piece of furniture. A range cooker or Aga will cope with large meals and offers flexibility for the keen cook (and electric Agas can be turned off, so are eco-friendly). There's one disadvantage: these freestanding pieces are bulky. But pick early on, and it's a case of tailoring the cabinetry to make that choice work. Likewise, if you long for a generous-sized sink, such as a ceramic Belfast/apron-front type or a deep marble style, factor it into the layout equation from day one.

In a small or streamlined kitchen, things are easier; you'll want an integrated refrigerator and freezer concealed behind cabinet doors.

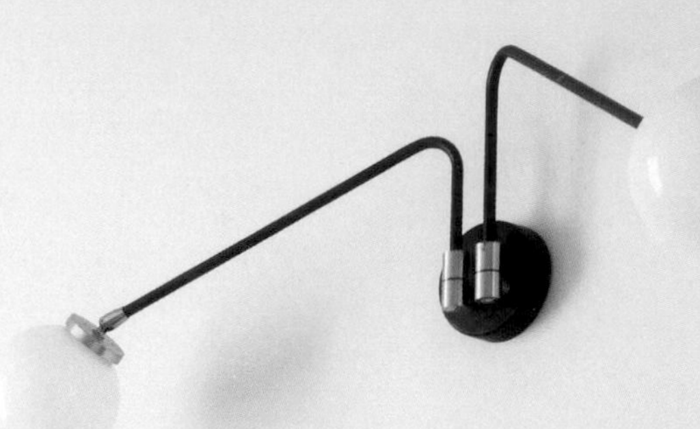

## THINK ABOUT
# ... LIGHTING

* For flexibility, hang small pendant or Edison-style filament bulb fittings on long cords/flexes; tuck them over ceiling hooks or drape across low beams. Fix multiple budget clamp lamps to bookshelves.

* Add colour pops with silk or linen drum shades lined with neon, black or gold. Use coloured cloth lamp cord/flex in either round or twisted options. Ribbed paper outsize lanterns are a bright budget choice.

* Clever placement looks chic. Instead of reading lights, suspend decorative pendant lamps low on each side of the bed or hang a giant sculptural light near a quiet armchair.

* Search for unique table lamps. Update 1960s and 1970s bases in Lucite, glazed ceramic or blown glass with new tall cylindrical, square or rectangular shades in zingy colours.

* Use multiples. Suspend several identical pendants over a kitchen island or a trio of contrasting shaped shades (or twinkling chandeliers) at varying heights above a table.

**OPPOSITE AND ABOVE** Let the history of a property nudge you towards a sympathetic design. In this old house, wood and stone materials feel authentic in the kitchen, yet the crisp cupboards are family-friendly. A chandelier creates a decorative link between the room's practical and sociable functions.

**ABOVE RIGHT** When a table doubles as an island unit, an L-shaped kitchen layout is a creative choice, gently wrapping around two sides of the key dining zone.

For built-in ovens, decide between single or double, a microwave and/or combination oven, either eye level or below countertop. Do you want the hob/cooktop close by, or located separately on an island unit? Investigating hobs/cooktops early makes it possible to weigh up extras, from a six-burner style to a wok attachment. In a minimal kitchen, you can get away with a cost-effective under-mounted stainless-steel sink, as it will 'disappear' beneath the worksurface. But remember that a tap/faucet silhouette will be on show, so make a conscious design decision: angular or curved?

However well appliances work, they must be aesthetically pleasing. As well as retro-style refrigerators, Agas and range cookers are also available in tempting colours from bubblegum pink to glossy brights. Nowadays it is possible to buy built-in ovens with sleek fascias in stainless or brushed steel, black, pastels or strong shades.

Equally early on, think about worksurfaces. All kitchen surfaces need to perform a double act; they must be functional but look amazing. Failsafe options that offer a good choice of both colour and textures include Corian, plus its more budget-conscious alternatives, composite stone and granite.

**ABOVE LEFT** In a small kitchen, planning cabinets right up to the ceiling looks tailored and maximizes storage space. Using white for the kitchen units and black for the breakfast cupboards marks a neat visual shift of boundaries.

**THIS PAGE** Colour and surface choices can transform a busy working kitchen into an enjoyable room. Custom-made leather stools are cheery and practical.

**OPPOSITE** It is no more complex to pick a patterned floor than plain. A graphic lino design adds richness to this interior.

**THIS PAGE** Pick the prettiest tableware for open shelves. Pendant lighting on extra-long cords/flexes makes an elegant alternative to spot task lighting.

**OPPOSITE ABOVE** Entertaining is easy if all the essentials are ready to go at a second's notice. Store condiments in beautiful containers and keep them out on display.

**OPPOSITE BELOW LEFT AND RIGHT** A galley kitchen must be rigorously planned. Use that ethos to dictate the styling, sticking to a monochrome scheme and straight lines.

Wood comes in every shade, from pale ash to dark iroko, while a reclaimed wooden worksurface will inject character. When you're picking a worksurface, ponder whether you want it to be the major visual focus in the room, such as a show-off expanse of swirled concrete. Or is it just one part of a cohesive theme, such as a black resin worktop with a matching floor?

For splashbacks, the balance of practicality versus star appeal alters subtly. They need to be wipe-clean, but you can also have some decorative fun. If you're after bold colour, then splashbacks are a brilliant vehicle for delivering it right at eye level. Plain square or subway-style tiles in a glossy black or tangerine are a good budget choice, or go for custom-made glass; specialist companies will match to Pantone references. In a relaxed kitchen, consider adding organic pattern in the splashback zone, using cement or encaustic tiles. Painting splashbacks a plain colour keeps costs down. Later on, as your budget allows, add a custom-made panel in stainless steel or copper.

We all know kitchen storage matters, but think through requirements in a logical way. Do an inventory of your existing possessions. Will they all fit? Can certain items be kept elsewhere, such as cleaning equipment in a utility room, perhaps? Work out if you're a cupboard or a shelf fan. If the former, streamlined options include a wall of floor-to-ceiling storage teamed with a kitchen island, or, for a mix-and-match look, a dresser/hutch and glazed cabinets. If the latter, will shelves be wall-mounted or floorstanding, slim or chunky? Some unsightly equipment should always be hidden away, so combine shelves with deep drawers. If you know, and understand, your storage requirements, planning the layout will become a breeze.

*** THINK AGAIN ...**
**and decorate with only two or three colours. It is a discipline, but looks visually neat for tiny flats and cohesive for open-plan spaces.**

**THIS PAGE** There is an art to designing built-in kitchen storage. In a relaxed kitchen, it shouldn't look too plain and uniform. Instead, tailor it to make the most of spare space and paint it to resemble a freestanding piece.

**OPPOSITE** Pendant lighting looks smart when perfectly positioned right above the kitchen table, but this needs early consideration. Lampshades are rich with all manner of decorative possibilities; use them to inject colour, texture or a vintage vibe.

This is all essential groundwork. Once it's done, celebrate, because you are poised to assemble the creative jigsaw. Now you can collect magazine tear sheets and visit kitchen showrooms. Hone choices by dividing kitchens into three style categories. A minimal look is functional and smart. Consider handle-free doors, gloss laminate or dark wood fascias, stone worksurfaces and built-in appliances. For a family-friendly kitchen, choose a relaxed mix of fitted cupboards and open shelves, painted units, reclaimed wood worktops and a lino floor. Or assemble freestanding appliances, timber or metal-fascia cupboard doors and concrete surfaces for a utility look. This style shorthand is merely a springboard. The more you experiment, the more confident you become.

And remember, your kitchen should remain a work in progress. Enjoy letting it evolve as paintings are hung, furniture chosen and atmospheric lighting added. The considered kitchen should appear effortless. Only you will know how much time has gone into making it work.

# THINK ...SITTING ROOMS

EXPERT THINKING

"Contrasts are effective. Try juxtaposing background neutrals with highlights of brighter, richer naturals. Colour adds great depth to an interior – and it is free."

**LUCY MARSTON**
*ARCHITECT*

We may entertain, read and watch television in the sitting room, but ultimately we really do retreat here to sit (or lounge, lie and curl up). So make this basic need the starting point for planning and decoration and ask some fundamental questions. What is the main focal point in this room? What are you going to sit on, look at, enjoy? And how do you want to feel here? Get these practical details right, and a relaxing, beautiful room will automatically follow on.

The key focal point in a sitting room is usually the fireplace, so make it a priority. If a chimney has been blocked, the flue must be checked before installing a

**LEFT** With floor-to-ceiling windows on two sides plus a fireplace, this room has a wealth of focal points. Therefore its seating is cleverly arranged in a square, providing vistas in all directions. To avoid a blocked-in look, matching sofas are twinned with a slim banquette and light rattan chairs.

**BELOW** Acknowledge the fact that you and your guests have time to linger in a sitting room. An exquisitely detailed tabletop will provide a sense of visual and tactile satisfaction.

new fire. Yes, it's an expense, but the introduction of flickering flames can radically improve the dynamics of any living space. Also, be brave enough to remove a mantelpiece if it's not right. Replacing a historically inappropriate style with an antique (or reproduction) surround, commissioning a modern marble mantelpiece or cladding the chimneybreast in wood panelling all deliver a stunning decorative focus. No fireplace? Try mirroring alcove walls

**THIS PAGE** In a knocked-through sitting room, it is critical to plan both halves so that the spaces look cohesive. In this townhouse, colour accents of powder blue, dove grey and hot pink neatly draw all corners together and add modern zip to the classical architecture.

**OPPOSITE** If you have a deep sash window, create a window seat and treat it in exactly the same way as a sofa, making it comfortable with luxurious upholstery and velvet cushions.

in antique-effect glass or adding a wall of floor-to-ceiling bookshelves. Diving in early and concentrating on a key focal point means you'll have ample budget and time to source (or commission) the perfect piece.

Be honest and accept that focal point number two will most likely be the television. It may be less glamorous, but it's crucial to decide where will it sit, naturally and neatly. If you're undertaking building work, plan now to 'lose' it within a wall recess, or frame it within timber cladding. Imagine you're watching a film, then follow your natural eyeline. Low is usually best, so avoid siting the screen unnaturally high above a fireplace. If you'd prefer to conceal the television, source a decorative piece of furniture and – even if it's not yet the time to install it – buy it now. A Chinese lacquered armoire or a vintage metal cabinet is capacious and looks attractive when closed.

Now concentrate on those crucial building blocks: pieces of upholstered furniture. Long before choosing styles, mull over the best layout, as this might also affect what look you go for. Is there space for two sofas, placed opposite or at right angles, or in a tiny room, might an L-shaped modular sofa suit better? In a narrow area, a long sofa teamed with twin armchairs, arranged in a U-shape, works brilliantly. For an open-plan zone, include low-slung leather armchairs or a buttoned ottoman, set apart from the main seating circle. Thinking through layouts means you know exactly what gaps to fill and it makes targeted shopping easier. Play around with positioning. Most rooms have a natural furniture arrangement that feels 'right'. So tap into your subconscious: do random jaunty angles or a linear set-up feel best?

Of course, choosing sofa and armchair styles and shapes is great fun. You can think about what works visually all you like, but there's no substitute for trying out real examples, working out the best balance of comfort, support

Lucian Freud Drawings
La collezione Peggy Guggenheim a Venezia

and visual appeal. But, simultaneously, project beyond those obvious factors of good looks and plumped-up comfort. Balance up short-term satisfaction versus long-term investment. Yes, a chain-store sofa is a cool, budget, quick-fix choice, but it may be more cost-effective to invest in a traditionally made piece, with a hand-jointed timber frame and feather and down cushions. Likewise, including vintage choices will provide your room with a layer of history and is eco-friendly. The effort it takes to source a good upholsterer to recover an antique armchair will be twinned with the knowledge that you're ending up with a customized, sublimely unique treasure.

Textile choices should come next, as their visual and tactile impact in a room is powerful. For years, we've been encouraged to choose self-effacing neutrals for upholstery.

**THIS PAGE** Artwork is often added late, but a show-stopping painting or a specially commissioned piece of decorative furniture needs consideration earlier on in the mix. Work out where it will hang or stand, then ensure it becomes a dazzling focal point by opting for spare, muted furnishings and accessories.

**OPPOSITE** If a scheme is based around one deep colour, layering tactile textures, from velvet upholstery to a wool or silk rug, adds a sense of richness and depth.

FASHION
ANNIE LEIBOVITZ A Photographer's Life 1990–2005
FASHION
audrey hepburn

**THIS PAGE AND OPPOSITE** A light, white sitting room is a treat by day, particularly if sun-drenched and with an enticing leafy vista beyond. But it must work as a cosy evening space, too. Avoid starkness by adding pops of hot colour, and pay attention to atmospheric night-time lighting. Choosing cocooning fabrics will help. Here, a fur throw, leather upholstery and a silk and wool rug, in cool winter whites, add softness.

But now there has been a sea change. Sofas and armchairs have become the stars, dressed up with jaunty geometrics and jewel shades. Rather than thinking in terms of one knockout pattern or colour, aim for eclectic, tactile contrasts. Broadly speaking, fabrics fall into key categories: crisp (linens, linen unions and cottons); textural (weaves, wool mixes, velvet); glamorous (silk, embroidered, satin) and hard-wearing (denim, hemp). Take a 'pick-and-mix' approach, adding one fabric from each category. A dash of gloss, from a Moroccan leather pouffe to a satin cushion, adds visual excitement. Of course, durability matters. But softness is crucial, too, because we all want comfort on the sofa.

By contrast, window treatments have morphed into the quiet 'sleepers' in a room scheme. Yet just because today's curtains and blinds are in plain, muted fabrics doesn't mean

# THINK ABOUT... UPHOLSTERY

* Be sparing but daring with a costly but beautiful print. Buy just enough fabric for dining chair seat pads and a matching drum lampshade overhead.
* Consider upholstery section by section. Sofa cushion squabs, armchair backs and dining chair seat and back supports can be upholstered separately in contrasting fabrics – plain with pattern or an identical print in several colourways.
* Be motif aware. Pick an abstract like a chevron or interlocking circles, source three fabrics echoing the pattern but mixing scales, textures and colours, then use for side chairs and a sofa. A strong motif holds everything together.
* Champion a young home-grown textile designer by choosing a new print each year. Add a fresh cushion as each collection is launched.
* Try colour-blocking on a dining chair or armchair. Use solid colour fabric for upholstery, then paint legs and arms to match. Add same-colour upholstery nails.

they should be an afterthought. It is all the more important that they be exquisitely made, and fulfil designated tasks, from unlined translucent blinds that provide privacy to interlined full-length curtains that add glamour and keep out draughts. Crisp detailing is essential so that everything looks a considered part of the whole. How to do that? Focus, just like a dressmaker, on the minutiae. A narrow scarlet band on the leading edge of plum mohair curtains, for example, or neutral linen blinds lined with a tiny bird-print cotton lawn (and adding a lampshade to match) will look incredibly chic.

**THIS PAGE** When planning a sitting room contained within a larger open-plan space, it is vital to choose beautifully shaped furniture with curvy contours; pieces that will naturally form a casual circle. This look is super-feminine, but kept sharp by upholstery in vibrant hues.

**THIS PAGE** An upholstered retro chair and stool is the ultimate multi-tasker. It's perfect for fireside relaxing, but pick one with a swivel base so that it links well with the formal sitting room, too.

**OPPOSITE** For a family sitting room, wall-to-wall fitted carpet is incredibly comfortable underfoot and adds warmth. A plain, light neutral feels crisp and modern, and wool fibres clean up easily. The same carpet used throughout all sociable areas maintains a tightly coordinated look.

Devote proper attention to cushions, as all too often they are amassed piecemeal long after a project is finished. Investing in show-off cushions can swiftly draw an entire room scheme together and pack a careful decorative punch. Choose quality duck-feather fillings, so cushions always look perky, and invest in luxuriously elegant fabrics, from velvet and silk to hand-printed cotton, or unusual textures, from shearling to ponyskin. Beautiful cushions don't come cheap. But, like quality buttons on a coat, they do make first impressions count.

Once these essentials are sorted, everything else, from lighting to occasional pieces, should be accumulated gradually. Don't be in a rush; composing and furnishing a room is an organic process. Live with your furniture and start using your sitting room. You'll soon spot gaps: the need for a third side table, a drinks trolley or a standard lamp. But look out for visual or tactile omissions, too. For example, if the room is in sombre colours and matt finishes, then the subtle glitter of a bronze-framed mirror will offer the perfect decorative fillip. If the look is grown-up elegance with sleek surfaces galore, then a lamp table in reclaimed timber will add an edgy dynamic. Art, rugs and lampshades are also clever vehicles for adding quirky, dense detail.

Smaller decorative accessories, from a 1950s glass collection to a beautiful handmade silk rug, offer the chance to layer essential individuality, because every sitting room should be personal. But focus on creating a tempting ambience, too. We can all begin to create that with candles and soft lighting. But real ambience also stems from a constantly shifting sense of stimulation within the room. So update decorative arrangements on a regular basis, and be open to adding fresh pieces and experimental influences. Get that stimulus right, and you've found the key to the perfectly thought-through sitting room.

**THIS PAGE** In a sitting room, every feature, however humble, must look its decorative best. Painting radiators to match walls helps blend them in. If possible, replace nondescript ones with cast-iron traditional styles. Treat them as furniture, perfect for propping up art.

**OPPOSITE** A wall of feature panelling is a brilliant choice in a family sitting room. Planned early on, it can house all manner of practicalities, from a built-in fireplace to a hidden TV or custom-built storage.

# THINK ...BEDROOMS

EXPERT THINKING

"Spending time on style or decorative internet sites and blogs can result in spectacular antique, reclaimed or high-street finds. And it makes international sourcing easy."

**SARAH DELANEY**
*INTERIOR DESIGNER*

MARTIN BRIL Vaarwel Eveline
100%
SASKIA NOORT

**OPPOSITE** In place of a dressing table, compose a feminine corner with a table for treasures and a full-length mirror.

**BELOW** It's a good idea to invest in stands and trays for displaying jewellery, scarves and shoes. Use them to create attractive (but controlled) still lifes around the room.

**RIGHT** Pare down the bed area. With its soaring ceiling, this attic bedroom needs little more than lighting and side tables to look beautiful.

We're often reminded that bedrooms should be tranquil and beautiful, to help us 'escape' the rigours of daily life. In reality, we're more likely to scoot through in an early morning rush, perhaps only truly enjoying the room's benefits on a weekend. For a bedroom to make us feel relaxed, even in those hurried moments, it needs to deliver a calm visual message. Your first priority is to tap into a soothing look that feels instinctive to you.

Go back to your notebook. This time, experiment with decorative word equations. Picture your ideal bedroom. Now note down a colour you love, a texture that appeals and a favourite motif. What mood, feeling or style does that sum up? What word did you write after the equals sign? One example might be powder blue + sand-blasted timber + garden foliage = fresh. Or charcoal + sheepskin + broad stripes = enveloping.

**THIS PAGE AND OPPOSITE** If there is the luxury of a picture window, bring the outside in and weave nature's colours into the bedroom scheme. In this new-build home, the shades of the landscape are brilliantly interpreted in a balanced composition of dark, light and mid-tones.

No-one else is going to see your word equation. It's not about coming up with right answers. But it does offer some first thoughts on a style.

Your second priority is to declutter, as a clear room feels airy and free. Make a conscious decision to furnish sparingly (but not sparsely) and review existing furniture. What immediate changes are possible? Perhaps a chest of drawers can be placed on the landing; clothes cupboards relocated to a spare room. If building work is in progress, section off a portion of the room with a stud wall for a walk-in closet. Floor-to-ceiling cupboards, painted to match the walls, look discreet. Keep doors flush, fitted with touch catches, or add handles in tactile leather, glass or bronze. For a decorative contrast, fit doors in beautifully grained wood, or finished with textured wallpaper. A full-length linen curtain is a glamorous wardrobe/closet-door alternative.

Of course, the bed will be the focus, but think of it from two viewpoints. Yes, it must look beautiful within the bedroom, but it should also guarantee comfort, a good view and tactile pleasure once lying in bed. So it's important to source a bed style that fulfils twin needs. Think of a divan with an upholstered headboard, from buttoned velvet to a plain linen cover, or a prettily carved vintage wood or French cane bed frame. Such choices deliver calming contours and a chic burst of colour into the room, while providing good support when you're in bed.

Mull over bed linen choices with a similar dual focus. Some linen and quilt choices look lovely on the bed, but are scratchy. So visit shops to feel potential bedding first. High thread-count Egyptian cottons, linens, either pre-washed or classic crisp variations, or silk all look and feel amazing. Think over colour and pattern. We're automatically programmed to pick white, as it is cool and fresh. But consider investing in a set of taupe, rose or china blue linens to give a little zip within the overall decorative scheme. For extras, think quality, not quantity. A cashmere, alpaca or merino wool blanket (or a satin eiderdown) is expensive, but it's also cosy, durable and beautiful. However simple the room, it will impart quiet luxury.

Revisit your word equations. What colours, textures and patterns have they prompted? Plain painted walls are great as they let busy minds zone out, while still allowing for dreamy colour.

**OPPOSITE AND ABOVE** Experiment by using natural light to inspire a colour scheme. Pick charcoal walls for a dark room; sugared almond pastels for a sunny attic.

**LEFT** However tiny the space, a bedroom chair is always practical. Choose a design classic for edgy glamour

THINK ABOUT

# ... STORAGE

* Take an inside-out approach and plan storage to include a visual surprise. Paint the interior of bookshelves a vibrant hue like leaf green or burnt orange, or hand-paint or fabric-line drawers in a sultry shade.

* Use unexpected materials for cupboard doors. Antique mirror panels, large-scale wallpaper, embossed leather or copper cladding all transform a humble built-in closet into a design feature.

* Play around with scale. Thick shelves give alcove storage a strong visual presence; the taller the ceiling, the wider and more dramatic you can go.

* Think through vertical and horizontal options. Will you pick one long shallow shelf running the length of a wall (brilliant for propped art, magazines or ceramics) or a stacked wall-mounted vertical bookshelf?

* Steal wall space from traffic areas, including the hall and corridors, for shallow bespoke bookshelves or coat cupboards. Have them lacquer spray-painted before fitting for a professional finish.

**THIS PAGE AND OPPOSITE** Actively link an en suite by decorating both rooms in identical colours. But switch the mood from restful to energetic by choosing plains in the bedroom, patterned tiles in the shower room.

**LEFT** Use spare space. Here, fitted cupboards have been 'sunk' into the wall of a corridor leading to the bedroom.

**RIGHT** Little details count. Plain linen Roman blinds are restful, but neat extras, like a bright contrast edging repeated on pillowcase embroidery or cushion piping, pull the whole room together.

**OPPOSITE** To add a punchy shade in the bedroom, but without overwhelming colour on walls, an upholstered headboard provides a glamorous contrast.

Deep shades, from teal to sage, are wonderfully soulful, especially teamed with floor-length and same-colour sheers or velvet curtains. Or take the colour across the floor in the form of a soft wool carpet in a vibrant hue. Used carefully, trailing leaf, geometric or bird-print patterns won't over-stimulate. Consider wallpapering only behind the bed or upholstering a headboard in a bright pattern. That way, you can enjoy the design by day, merely glimpsing it once in bed.

The perfect relaxing bedroom fuses pared-down purity with real beauty. So avoid too many accessories or over-cluttering walls. A stunning picture, or a cleverly considered arrangement of paintings, creates a natural focus above the bed. But it's important to provide visual inspiration on waking, too. If you're blessed with a country view, then position the bed to see out of the window and fit blinds, rather than curtains, to maximize the vista. Otherwise, hang something lovely opposite the bed. An abstract painting is soothing, as is a fine art photograph of a landscape, foliage or the sea. For a really pure space, use mirrors to capture light and reflections. Try cladding wardrobe/closet doors with antique-effect mirrors. Experiment with a large vintage mirror as a headboard, or decorate the bedhead wall with panels of *verre églomisé* silver-gilded glass.

As for the remaining furniture, keep things simple. Choose unobtrusive bedside tables, from a 1960s-style drawer unit to a circular lamp table. In a modern bedroom, pick a floating shelf or a wall-hung cube, perhaps in a bright lacquer. Keep surfaces clear, if possible, by wall-mounting reading lamps. Is there space for an armchair, small sofa or a low cushioned bench for quiet moments? Pick tactile upholstery, from a wool/cashmere weave to crisp linen. A dressing table is always a treat. Choose one with a neat, tailored silhouette, perhaps in oak or walnut, and don't over-clutter it.

GRACE
Henry Cecil
NELSON

# THINK ...BATHROOMS

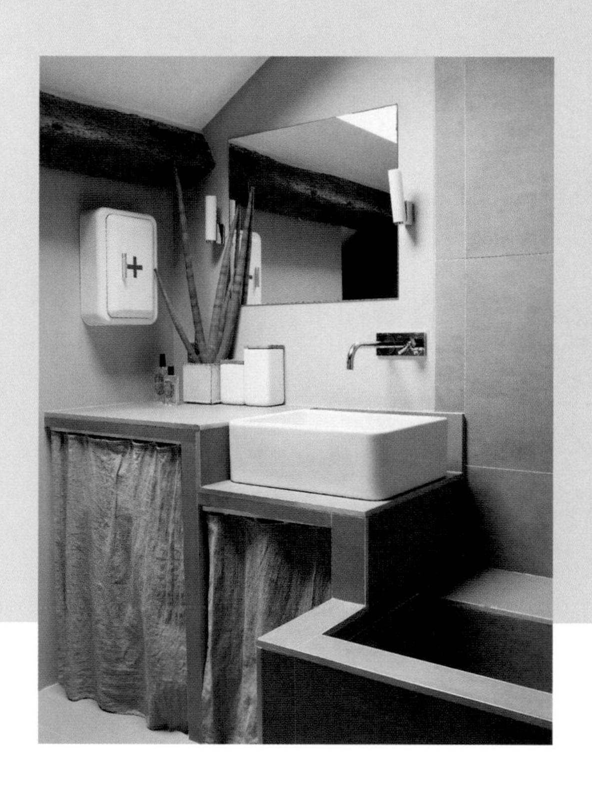

**EXPERT THINKING**

"A bathroom must be as functional as possible for adults and children, so a custom-made shower/bathtub works well. A good bathroom should be pure, bright, tactile and warm."

**ISABELLE JUY**
*ARCHITECT*

**OPPOSITE** In a large bathroom, choose decorative pieces to add height, as most bathroom fittings stop at waist level. Here, a vintage cabinet and a chandelier glamorously fill the space.

**ABOVE** Consider tucking away the shower and toilet beyond the main bathroom, using a partition wall or sliding doors. This creates a neat division between wash zone and shower space.

**ABOVE RIGHT** Run your chosen textural contrasts right through to accessories. Distressed wood and rattan mix with glossy marble and natural shells.

A bathroom must combine functionality with good looks, but as a result, we often plan it in isolation. Frequently, this means a bathroom misses out on strong decorative themes used in other rooms. Resolve to plan and furnish it to make it feel linked to your living spaces. The bathroom is a very private space, so give yourself carte blanche. Tap into your imagination and create something amazing.

First, ask the key questions. Who will use it? Is this an en suite or a family room? What is your preference: a slick shower room or a luxurious retreat? Upgrade plumbing early. A booster pump to improve water pressure, a heated towel rail/rod and underfloor heating will all transform efficiency. Does the space pose any restrictions? A sloping ceiling, say, may dictate a bathtub rather than a shower. What changes might be possible? A large bathroom may offer the potential for a partition wall to section off a toilet or a floating wall to conceal a walk-in shower.

Designing a bathroom is exacting, as you can't plan organically stage by stage. Decisions must be made in tandem, so the sanitaryware can be installed and the pipework concealed prior to surfaces being tiled or clad.

*** THINK STRAIGHT ...**
**but not necessarily vertical. Use textured wallpapers, tongue-and-groove cladding and patterned fabrics horizontally.**

**THIS PAGE** Good taps/faucets are an investment, but think of them as quality accessories. Touch and try them to work out what suits your sanitaryware, decoratively and practically. Will taps/faucets be wall- or deck-mounted, pillar styles or part of a bathtub/shower mixer? Finishes include chrome, polished or brushed nickel plated or antique brass or gold. Shower mixer plates may be square or circular.

**OPPOSITE** Tongue-and-groove panelling is cost-effective yet super-smart, useful for hiding pipes and can be tailored to the ideal height for a shelf. Paint it in a vibrant shade to personalize white sanitaryware.

**THIS PAGE** Bring natural light into the shower. In this clever en-suite enclosure, glass panels direct sunlight via the bedroom. Alternatively, locate the shower next to a window glazed with frosted glass, or close to a skylight.

**OPPOSITE** You'll see the shower every morning, so make it upbeat. Pick tiles in a vibrant colour and scale; boldly use them right across the floor and up the wall. Modern cement tiles come in snazzy geometric designs.

Often, we obsess over bathroom fittings and pick decoration at the last minute. If you fancy coloured sanitaryware, then investigate first. Otherwise, reverse your thinking and focus on surfaces. They cover large expanses, so have a powerful decorative influence. A burst of colour looks gorgeous in a bathroom. Can it be delivered via floor-to-ceiling porcelain tiles or walls painted in warm tobacco or hot coral? If glamour is paramount, will mother-of-pearl tiling fit the bill?

Consider whether you'll be incorporating built-in storage before walls are finished. An inset alcove within a shower zone, ceramic-tiled to match the wall, or a mirrored bathroom cupboard sunk into the wall above a basin gives a polished finish. What about taps/faucets? For wall- or pillar-mounted styles, plumbing needs to be done before surfaces are added.

With early choices made, consider the jigsaw of how to use them. Think big. Don't restrict tiles to a small splashback area or the shower enclosure. It is smarter to take them right

**OPPOSITE** Irregular proportions can be the catalyst for solutions. Here, a sloping ceiling has prompted a tailored design for a secluded built-in bathtub, with the sink located in the full-height section of the room. Pick one or two versatile materials that can be used over all surfaces – polished loam and tongue and groove work brilliantly here – to create a tight, cohesive look.

**THIS PAGE** If wall space is lacking, consider alternative storage to the ubiquitous bathroom cabinet. Is it possible to build in a cabinet below a vanity worktop? Can towels be stacked on low-level shelves? A selection of rattan baskets, ceramic containers or pretty glass jars can hold bathroom essentials.

across one wall. Tongue and groove, a favourite for bathtub panels, gives a pulled-together look if used all over a bathroom. Now think connections. Do you want contrast or cohesion? The deliberate juxtaposition of two different surfaces, like a wall of tiny silver glass mosaics and large matt slate floor tiles, looks dramatic. But for a calmer look, pick a material that works both vertically and horizontally, like concrete, limestone or marble.

Increasingly there is a pick-and-mix attitude towards bathroom fittings. Think of tubs or basins as eclectic pieces of furniture, with decorative surfaces as the cohesive link. Beyond classic freestanding roll-top tubs, consider the elegant, simple lines of early-20th-century styles. In a large room, try fixing the bathtub centre-stage. A big tub will feel luxurious (and wonderfully snug) in a tiny bathroom. Just tailor the remaining space carefully. For a streamlined look, pick a rectangular bath, cladding the surround to match key surfaces. If budget fittings are a necessity, expensive taps/faucets in a quality finish like satin nickel, give an instant upgrade. Quirky reclaimed antique taps/faucets will deflect attention, too.

For shower choices, delve beyond the obvious. Might an open shower be incorporated at one end of a family bathroom, with a drain in a tiled floor? Can you knock through into an adjacent room and fit the shower into the borrowed space, the entry point flush with the bathroom wall? A floor-to-ceiling toughened glass screen allows for greater light flow within a room. A frosted glass screen is a more modest option. In a traditional bathroom, linen or a coloured-print shower curtain with a waterproof lining looks chic.

Once your bathroom is installed, those early thought processes will reward you with an effortless room and everything in the right place. Don't stop there. The addition of one unexpected decorative item can leapfrog your bathroom into the next league. Whether it's a vintage mirror, a piece of art or a show-off chandelier, go for bold scale and textural contrast.

**THIS PAGE** Tailor a family shower room to appeal to all ages. For a wetroom-style shower, good anti-slip flooring choices include textural slate, or pebble mosaics, which are fun for children and feel amazing underfoot. Choose a simple shower mixer that everyone can operate, and fit an energy-efficient showerhead to reduce water flow – a good idea for kids.

# THINK ...WORK & PLAY ROOMS

EXPERT THINKING

"A peaceful workplace has to feel like home, so don't make it too businesslike."

**JUDITH KRAMER**
*ARTIST/INTERIOR DESIGNER*

Visual charades. What has an ox to do with the
letter A? The art of looking sideways. How to turn
knots into bows. When does
Why sit with your back to the view? Notes on the

**OPPOSITE** Create a family version of office hot-desking with a central table and plenty of chairs. This is a good way to multi-task a separate dining room, using it as a work room by day; entertaining zone by night. Provide sufficient storage for tidying away files and technology.

**LEFT** Instead of office-style shelves, invest in custom-built cabinets for papers and books. Black, grey or plum painted joinery is more sophisticated than white.

**BELOW** Mix in decorative elements to please all ages, from framed kids' art to chairs upholstered in city stripes.

Many of us work from home, kids and adults alike, regularly or on an ad hoc basis. So it's good to have a spot for the computer, files and books. Unlike a serious home office, though, picture the ideal work room as an inviting space. Make it's easy-access, adjacent to the kitchen or close by in a hall, and it will get daily use. If a family member needs peace, it's no longer necessary to work away from noise: use headphones. Aim to create a shared room for work and play so that everyone gravitates here.

Catering for mixed needs means designing a multi-stranded room. It must be practical. Most work rooms will be small, or a purpose-built zone situated within a corridor or a landing. Think neat. Built-in cupboards, a wall-mounted worksurface or a window-seat bench are all space-savers. Either custom-build fittings, or buy chain-store storage and customize it with paint. For serious working, provide a wide surface so that several people can sit together, with a painted, wood or zinc top. This doesn't have to be a desk — a plain trestle or a long vintage pine dining table will do.

# THINK ABOUT ... ART

* Ignore symmetry. Hang one painting slightly off-centre above a mantelpiece or position pictures one above another in a single alcove, leaving the remaining alcove bare. Group massed paintings together, but without lining them up perfectly.

* Refresh traditional landscapes or portraits by reworking them in matt black frames with no mount. A slim surround, in neon-painted wood, looks modern.

* Reverse white gallery-style walls. Paint one wall in black, charcoal or chartreuse and hang a mix of paintings in contrasting sizes and shapes. Modern art looks stunning hung against crisp wood panelling.

* Think minimal. Hanging one vast modern photograph or oil, while keeping other walls bare, has double the power of multiple pictures. And think placement. Hung low, an eye-catching artwork can define a separate seating or desk area.

* Confidently overlap art with furniture. Butting up a sofa or desk against a giant painting gives a chic yet nonchalant finish.

**THIS PAGE** In a large play/TV room, consider arranging a quiet desk area in one corner. The work surface doesn't have to be vast; a vintage school desk or a painted table would suffice. Positioning matters. This one is close to natural daylight, equipped for evening homework with a task lamp.

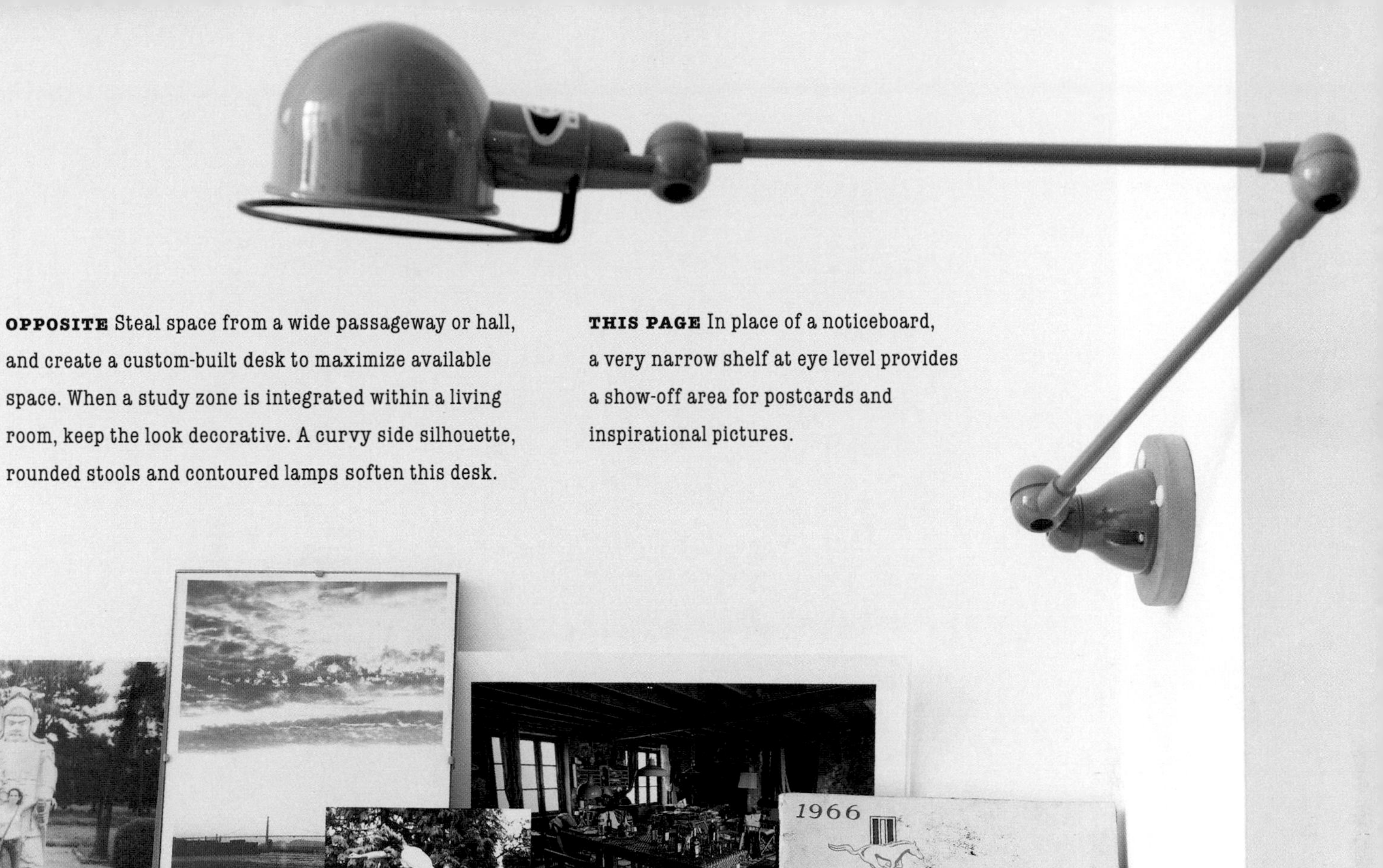

**OPPOSITE** Steal space from a wide passageway or hall, and create a custom-built desk to maximize available space. When a study zone is integrated within a living room, keep the look decorative. A curvy side silhouette, rounded stools and contoured lamps soften this desk.

**THIS PAGE** In place of a noticeboard, a very narrow shelf at eye level provides a show-off area for postcards and inspirational pictures.

**THIS PAGE** Providing a purpose-built play area keeps the rest of your home streamlined, and, because structures will be small-scale, makes inspired use of awkward spaces. A playhouse can look cool if planned as an integral part of the decorative scheme.

A work/play space should also feel stimulating and creative. How to please everyone? Don't ask the family for practical requirements (that would be boring). Instead, get them to compile a 'top five' list of fun items and build your scheme around it. If that includes a banana yellow swivel chair, sea green wall or a polka dot rug, then you're going in the right direction. Decorating with one eye on the whimsical is fun and makes for a really personal space. Search out wallpapers depicting everything from ski scenes to retro telephones, pictorial rugs and abstract, upbeat art. Remember the key components here: work space, chair, lamp. Choose colourful, quirky, user-friendly examples so that people want to use them.

Aside from the obvious homework and computer use, second-guess other activities and equip the space accordingly. For reading, you could add an armchair. Look out for funky modern versions of the classic wing chair (upholstered in a strong colour like chartreuse) or cover a floor mattress in practical denim stripes. Toy storage for an adult/kid's room must look more sophisticated than plastic containers. Options such as wicker baskets on castors, vintage fruit crates with an upholstered seat or felt boxes are smart. And if you choose good-looking storage, then it won't need to be tidied away.

**ABOVE** Perfectly positioned lighting elevates a simple play zone into a snappily designed room that adults can enjoy, too. Plan with an eye to the future; smart lighting to match artwork will endure after the play house has gone.

**RIGHT** A multifunctional noticeboard is a brilliant decorative addition. Turn it into a dynamic learning tool; this one features a world map made from plastic bottletops.

**OPPOSITE** Imaginative touches don't have to be show-off statements. This bi-fold door leading into a kitchen is glazed in sections of antiqued mirror. When shut, it gives the illusion of a freestanding mirror.

**BELOW** It's easier to experiment with neon or hot colours if using just one chair or table. Budget choices ensure the chance to ring the changes.

**RIGHT** Artworks are a clever shortcut to reinforcing a colour palette. In this new-build home, an oil painting reflects nature's hues outside the window.

# CONCLUSION: CREATIVE THINKING

Most of us, when asked to engage in 'creative thinking', will freeze up. But creative thinking is not about having ground-breaking ideas or devising unusual colour combinations. It concerns freeing up thoughts so that we feel bold enough to experiment. Cultivating a 'what if?' attitude is liberating and fun. Start small and think big. If you begin with occasional twists – trying one neon vase in a pastel room, or propping up a modern painting on a traditional fireplace – only you will witness any mistakes. More likely, they will be triumphs. The more you succeed, the more fun decorating will become.

Think like a stylist. Good styling is about customizing and showing familiar things in a new way. If you're briefing a soft furnishings maker, have the confidence to ask for specific yet subtle details. You might want wide satin ribbon at the base of a plain curtain, a colourful frill around a neutral chair cover or a chevron-patterned contrasting seat cushion. If you are enthusiastic and experimental, a good maker will engage with your creativity. They may offer new ideas, too. Many furniture companies give the chance to customize finishes, sizing or colours. So if the option you have in mind isn't listed, ask the question. There may be a charge, but isn't that worthwhile if it means that you achieve a unique piece?

Lose the fear. Worrying whether a fabric will look right made up as curtains, or if a colour works in a bedroom, can stifle creative thoughts. No-one wants to make expensive mistakes. But not venturing out occasionally with an exciting pattern or colour can result in a bland interior. Work in layers. Start with one navy wall, or a large-scale patterned headboard, or a solo bright tangerine armchair. Live with it. And if it's working, add more.

Know your sources. Many of us increase outings to design stores, look at websites and read interiors magazines to amass inspiration. But make a concerted effort to use this research time to widen your range of specialists, shops and suppliers, too. (Interior designers are always on the hunt.) Track down wholesale fabric suppliers with exciting rough linens or wool suitings, an up-and-coming wallpaper designer with a launch collection, a wonderful trimmings shop or a bespoke lampshade maker. Investigate sources overseas; enjoy that journey online. The more choices, the easier it is to dream up a creative scheme.

Break the rules. The most eye-catching looks can stem from little changes. Use a vintage wall light as a ceiling pendant, upholster an armchair using the fabric inside out or paint a ceiling black and a floor white rather than the other way around. Challenge accepted thought processes. The received wisdom is to invest in beautiful soft furnishings and choose wall coverings to last, accessorizing with inexpensive, trend-led extras. Consider trying the opposite. Use simple, budget wallcoverings and upholster sofas in plain cottons. Then spend your money on a glorious hand-crafted designer cushion, or a bespoke rug and a striking piece of art. How does that design ethos feel?

And don't wait. It's true that decorating a home is always an expense. Often it feels necessary to live with a sofa in need of re-covering, while you carefully save up. But we look at our homes every single day. Is it possible to do some creative accounting? What might you have to give up, realistically, to make just one change for the better? We are emotional creatures, deeply affected by our surroundings. Don't you deserve to live in a cleverly planned, neatly executed and beautifully finished space?

**ABOVE** Enjoy looking for patterns, shapes or colour links to creatively bind together a scheme. Here, twisty armchair silhouettes echo the table legs (left), the graphic regularity of the artwork is repeated in the lamp (centre) and the glossy drum shade mimics the circular side table (right).

**OPPOSITE** Adding a flash of unexpected colour to a monochrome scheme doesn't have to mean using brights. Warm, muted shades, included on a cushion cover, book spines or an occasional table, will still 'lift' a subtle scheme.

Gandhi
GYPSET TRAVEL
VINTAGE T-SHIRTS
balichic
SURFING
TASCHEN
ALFRESCO
NIGELLA EXPRESS
barefoot contessa back to basics
Moroccan Interiors
TASCHEN

# SOURCES

## ONE-STOP STYLE SHOPS

**Anthropologie**
158 Regent Street
London W1B 5SW
020 7529 9800
www.anthropologie.eu
Inspirational, fashion-led home accessories, including pictorial wallpaper, colourful rugs, quirky furniture and lighting.

**The Conran Shop**
Michelin House
81 Fulham Road
London SW3 6RD
020 7589 7401
www.conranshop.co.uk
Contemporary designer furniture and furnishings, including an excellent selection of modern lighting.

**Graham & Green**
4 Elgin Crescent
London W11 2HX
020 7243 8908
www.grahamandgreen.co.uk
Wide choice of furniture including velvet-upholstered sofas and armchairs, side tables, pouffes, mirrors and covetable accessories.

**Heals**
196 Tottenham Court Road
London W1T 7LQ
020 7636 1666
www.heals.co.uk
Modern and designer furniture, lighting and bed/bath linens with an emphasis on simplicity and quality.

**Holly's House**
283 New Kings Road
London SW6 4RD
020 7736 2222
www.hollys-house.com
Quirky selection of modern and vintage furniture, graphic rugs and accessories, plus an inspired selection of textured and pictorial wallpapers.

**Mint**
2 North Terrace
Alexander Square
London SW3 2BA
020 7225 2228
www.mintshop.co.uk
Cool interior design shop with a carefully curated mix of stylish, elegant furniture and home accessories from international sources. Interior design consultation service, too.

**OKA**
www.okadirect.com
Chic, classic furniture for every room, plus a vast choice of decorative lighting, cushions and occasional tables.

## PAINT

**Colour and Paint**
www.colourandpaint.com
Online paint retailer of designer brands, including Mr & Mrs Smith and Liberty Paint.

**Dulux**
www.dulux.co.uk
Enormous selection of paint colours, including timeless classic shades and strong colours suitable for feature walls.

**Farrow & Ball**
www.farrow-ball.com
Huge choice of inspirational paints arranged according to colour groups, or pale, mid- and strong shades. Colour consultancy service available.

**Little Greene**
www.littlegreene.com
Beautiful paint ranges grouped according to historical periods, neutrals, 1960s-1970s and an entire grey collection, plus retro wallpapers.

**Sanderson**
www.sanderson-uk.com
A large designer paint collection with 140 shades, including good moody colours and a selection of strong brights.

**Zoffany**
Design Centre Chelsea Harbour
Lots Road
London SW10 0XE
0844 543 4748
www.zoffany.com
Classy designer range of 128 deep and neutral paints in flat emulsion and eggshell, including good purples, grey and deep blue.

## WALLPAPER

**Cole & Son**
www.cole-and-son.com
Traditional wallpaper specialists reinvented with cool modern-day collections like Geometrics and Vivienne Westwood, plus classics from the 1950s and '60s. Bespoke custom colour service also available.

**Neisha Crosland**
www.neishacrosland.com
Large-scale, modern organic, striped and graphic print wallpapers in subtle shades. Also terracotta tiles in the designer's signature triangles and dots, plus decorative hand-finished leather tiles.

**Graham & Brown**
www.grahambrown.com
Vast array of cost-effective wallpapers specializing in contemporary designs and geometrics, including designer ranges by Wayne Hemingway and Kelly Hoppen.

**Harlequin**
www.harlequin.uk.com
Imaginative wallpapers and coordinating fabrics, many with a retro spin or large-scale organic patterns.

**Mini Moderns**
www.minimoderns.com
Own-design wallpapers with a wide choice of graphic designs, including retro chairs, Festival of Britain and houses feature papers. Rugs, cushions and fabrics, too.

**Scion**
www.scion.uk.com
Contemporary British furnishings brand with wallpapers and fabrics in breezy colours and geometric patterns.

## FABRIC

**Designers Guild**
267-277 Kings Road
London SW3 5EN
020 7351 5775
www.designersguild.com
Inspirational fabrics; prints, upholstery weaves, velvets, dyed cottons and linens in huge range of pale and vibrant colours. Also coordinating wallpapers, upholstery, bed/bath and rugs.

**Fermoie**
2 Pond Place
London SW3 6QJ
01672 513723
www.fermoie.com
Beautiful British-made fabrics presented in colour 'groups' offering plain linens and cottons, weaves and stripes. Also lampshades and cushions in coordinating fabrics.

**Osborne & Little**
304 Kings Road
London SW3 5UH
020 7352 1456
www.osborneandlittle.com
Stylish designer fabrics, including collections by designers Nina Campbell and Matthew Williamson. Great for inventive weaves and a vast range of plains.

**Rapture & Wright**
www.raptureandwright.co.uk
British linens, linen unions and wool upholstery fabrics in deep and nature-inspired hues, printed with contemporary organic motifs and geometrics. Wallpapers, lampshades and own-range sofas, too.

**St Judes Fabrics**
www.stjudesfabrics.co.uk
Artist-designed British screen-printed fabrics, offering a modern take on traditional nature motifs plus designs with a retro vibe. Matching lampshades, blankets, wallpapers and accessories.

**Timorous Beasties**
46 Amwell Street
London EC1R 1XS
(by appointment only)
020 7833 5010
www.timorousbeasties.com
Fabulously imaginative own-design fabrics with everything from insects and birds, on linen or velvet, plus modern-day toile de Jouy . Also rugs, cushions and pattern-lined drum lampshades.

## TILES & STONE

**Fired Earth**
www.firedearth.com
Huge selection of tiles including terracotta, slate, stone, porcelain and ceramics, neutral and bright colours. An excellent paint collection, plus contemporary and classic kitchen and bathroom fittings.

**Lapicida**
533 Kings Road
London SW10 0TZ
020 3355 5598
www.lapicida.com
International natural stone specialists, with stones from marble to limestone, terracotta to onyx. Design service available.

**Mandarin Stone**
www.mandarinstone.com
Over 100 different lines of inspiring limestone, marble, travertine, slate and basalt, plus decorative and glazed tiles and stone sinks and basins.

**Popham Design**
www.pophamdesign.com
Vibrant, modern graphic and squiggly organic motif cement tiles handmade in Morocco.

**Stonell**
www.stonell.com
Specialists in natural stone, supplying everything from limestone and basalt to marble and travertine. Stone basins, sinks and shower trays too.

**Stone Age**
www.stone-age.co.uk
Natural stone flooring, including antiqued flooring, stone basins and fire surrounds. Granite and marble in an inspiring range of different colours.

**Surface Tiles**
60 Queenstown Road
London SW8 3RY
020 7819 2301
www.surfacetiles.com
Huge choice of stone, porcelain and glass tiles and natural wood, arranged according to 'moods' from contemporary to luxury.

**Topps Tiles**
www.toppstiles.co.uk
Vast selection of budget kitchen and bathroom tiles, including unusual porcelain tiles to resemble wood grain, bright subway-style tiles and marble.

## WOOD

**Kahrs**
www.kahrs.com
Affordable timber flooring in oak, maple and walnut, with finishes that range from brushed to smoked.

**Natural Wood Floor**
20 Smugglers Way
London SW18 1EQ
020 8871 9771
www.naturalwoodfloor.co.uk
Engineered and solid wood flooring, parquet floors and high-quality solid wood kitchen worksurfaces.

**Solid Floor**
61 Paddington Street
London W1U 4JD
020 7486 4838
www.solidfloor.co.uk
Solid wood or engineered board flooring in many textures, including reclaimed-effect, brushed, smooth and hand-scraped. Waxed, stained and oiled finishes.

**Walking on Wood**
490 Kings Road
London SW10 0LF
020 7352 7311
www.walkingonwood.com
Bespoke handmade parquet wood flooring in oak, walnut, wenge and more. Bespoke patterns available or combinations with leather, steel and glass.

## CONCRETE/RESIN & POLISHED PLASTER

**Lazenby**
www.lazenby.co.uk
Experts in polished concrete flooring and worktops, available in a choice of different colours and finishes.

**The Resin Floor Company**
www.resinflooringcompany.com
Poured resin flooring in a wide range of colours, polished concrete, and stone 'carpets'.

**Surface Form**
www.surfaceform.com
Specialists in polished plaster floors and worksurfaces in a wide range of colours and finishes, including pitted plaster and marmorino. Also polished concrete.

## UNUSUAL SURFACES

**Decorum Est**
568 Kings Road
London SW6 2DY
020 7731 5556
www.decorumest.com
Internationally sourced selection of exotic and unusual surface materials, including marble, stone and concrete, precious metals, shells and glass.

**De Ferranti**
583 Kings Road
London SW6 2EH
020 7384 4424
www.deferranti.com
An Aladdin's cave of luxurious surfaces, including shellwork, rare limestone, leather, metal tiles and lava.

**Element 7**
Unit 2
Parsons Green Depot
Parsons Green Lane
London SW6 4HH
020 7736 2366
www.element7.co.uk
Exotic range of metal, leather, parquet and wide plank flooring, all supplied with radiant underfloor heating.

**Fameed Khalique**
Unit 101
190 St John Street
London EC1V 4JY
020 7490 5524
www.fameedkhalique.com
An internationally sourced exquisite collection of surfaces including leather, aluminium, semiprecious stones, conglomerate glass combinations and hide rugs.

**Retrouvius**
1016 Harrow Road
London NW10 5NS
020 8960 6060
www.retrouvius.com
Eclectic architectural salvage materials, including stone, metalwork and timber surfaces, plus vintage furniture and lighting, mirrors, doors, panelling and fireplaces.

**Rough Old Glass**
2 Home Farm Buildings
Lower Blakewell
Muddiford
Devon EX31 4ET
0845 548 8586
(by appointment only)
www.rougholdglass.co.uk
Restoration and conservation specialists offer antiqued mirror glass panels and tiles to order.

**Dominic Schuster**
Studio F160
Riverside Business Centre
Haldane Place
London SW18 4UQ
(by appointment only)
020 8874 0762
www.dominic-schuster.com
Specialists in antiqued mirror glass in a choice of finishes including old silver, fossil gold and heavy mercury. Also colour tinted and *verre églomisé* options.

**WorkHouse**
63-65 Princelet Street
London E1 5LP
020 7247 1815
www.workhousecollection.co.uk
Company specialising in hand-crafted products, including 200 patterned/coloured cement tiles from Tangiers. Also steel-framed internal partition doors.

## KITCHENS & APPLIANCES

**Aga**
www.agaliving.com
Aga range cookers in a choice of fuels plus electric, and conventional cookers, all in tempting colours.

**DeVOL**
01509 261000
www.devolkitchens.co.uk
Own-brand classic, Shaker style and modern timber kitchens, with a choice of granite, marble or oak worktops.

**Ikea**
www.ikea.co.uk
Wide range of budget kitchens in classic and modern styles, including base and wall cabinets, doors and handles.

**John Lewis**
www.johnlewis.com
Quality built-in kitchens plus appliances. Inspiring selection of built-in coloured ovens and fridges.

**Plain English**
28 Blandford Street
London W1U 4BZ
020 7486 2674
www.plainenglishdesign.co.uk
Beautifully made, simply styled bespoke kitchens in painted finishes. Colours for Cupboards is their own-brand paint range in 12 bright and muted shades.

**Rangemaster**
www.rangemaster.co.uk
Classic British freestanding range cookers, in a wide choice of colours, plus appliances and sink and tap ranges.

**Smeg**
www.smeguk.com
Fridges and fridge-freezers in classic and retro styles, every colour from lime green to pastels.

**Superfront**
www.superfront.com
Ingenious company offering modern, beautiful door fronts and handles, smart designs and colours, to fit Ikea kitchens, and selected other furniture.

## FURNITURE

**Amy Somerville**
Leeder House
6 Erskine Road,
London NW3 3AJ
020 7586 2211
www.amysomerville.com
Super-chic, beautifully made furniture including desks, side tables and sofas, many with jewel coloured upholstery. Small, select rug and fabric collection.

**Another Country**
www.anothercountry.com
Simply styled, contemporary furniture, including sleek modern daybeds, desks and stools.

**A T Cronin**
020 8749 2995
www.atcronin.co.uk
London-based workshop offering beautifully made classic furniture, including the Virginia White Collection of traditional designs with a modern twist. Leatherwork and wall upholstery too.

**Bethan Gray**
www.bethangray.com
British designer offering a quirky modern take on traditional furniture: side and coffee tables feature marble tops or leather bases.

**Keir Townsend**
142 Old Brompton Road
London SW7 4NR
020 7746 2442
www.keirtownsend.com
A hand-picked selection of modern furniture and lighting, featuring unusual finishes such as burnished copper or glossy steel coffee tables.

**Loaf**
0845 468 0698
www.loaf.com
Affordable, contemporary sofas, beds, tables and bathroom and kitchen accessories. Configurations include modular and corner designs.

**Made.com**
Ninth Floor
Newcombe House
45 Notting Hill Gate
London, W11 3LQ
0845 557 6888

www.made.com

Online store with a wide range of smart, contemporary designer furniture direct to the customer.

**Ochre**
46-47 Britton Street
London EC1M 5UJ
020 7096 7372

www.ochre.net

Modern furniture and lighting, specialising in oversized curved, modular and corner sofas, occasional tables and breathtakingly beautiful modern chandeliers.

**Pinch**
Unit1W
Clapham North Art Centre
26-32 Voltaire Road
London SW4 6DH
(by appointment only)
020 7622 5075

www.pinchdesign.com

Gloriously simple but beautifully designed contemporary furniture, including slim sideboards, benches, desks and upholstery.

**George Smith**
587-589 Kings Road
London SW6 2EH
020 7384 1004

www.georgesmith.co.uk

Traditionally crafted classic sofas, armchairs and chaises, plus cowhide, leather and kilim upholstery options.

**Sofa.com**
0845 400 2222

www.sofa.com

Affordable range of bespoke sofas with vast choice of fabric upholstery and every style from modular sofas to loveseats, plus chaises and footstools.

**Rose Uniacke**
76-78 Pimlico Road
London SW1W 8PL
020 7730 7050

www.roseuniacke.com

Elegant own-design furniture including occasional tables and sofas, lighting and cashmere blankets.

## LIGHTING

**Holloways of Ludlow**
121 Shepherds Bush Road
London W6 7LP
020 7602 5757

www.hollowaysofludlow.com

Large selection of contemporary lighting, including industrial steel and blown glass pendant lights, plus switches and sockets.

**Original BTC**
Design Centre Chelsea Harbour
Lots Road
London SW10 0XE
020 7351 2130

www.lightingmatters.co.uk

British-made lighting in everything from bone china to metal.

**Skinflint Design**

www.skinflintdesign.co.uk

Reclaimed 20th-century lighting, including warehouse pendant lights and vintage machinist task lighting.

**Trainspotters**

www.trainspotters.co.uk

Industrial and salvage lighting, including enamelled pendant lights in bright colours and outsize factory lights.

**Urban Cottage Industries**

www.urbancottageindustries.com

Vintage shades, filament light bulbs, twisted and straight traditional lighting cables in many colours from neon green to pink. Also wire bulb cages.

## BATHROOMS

**Aston Matthews**
141-147a Essex Road
London N1 2SN
020 7226 7220

www.astonmatthews.co.uk

A comprehensive selection of bathroom fittings including freestanding baths, basins, taps and showers, modern and traditional.

**Balineum**

www.balineum.co.uk

Chic bathroom accessories including cotton/linen, pique and gauzy linen shower curtains, bathroom storage baskets and Egyptian cotton towels.

**Drummonds**
78 Royal Hospital Road
London SW3 4HN
020 7376 4499

www.drummonds-uk.com

Cast-iron freestanding baths with specialist finishes including concrete or antique bronze. Also classic basins, WCs, showers and bathroom lights.

**CP Hart**

www.cphart.co.uk

Modern to traditional bathroom fittings, including freestanding and inset baths, basins, designer taps and a wide variety of tiles and surfaces.

**Healey and Lord**
01603 488709

www.healeyandlord.com

Suppliers of specialist sanitaryware, including black bathroom collections and even leather-effect bathrooms.

**The Water Monopoly**
10-14 Lonsdale Road
London NW6 6RD
020 7624 2636

www.thewatermonopoly.com

Beautiful freestanding classic bath styles, including Empire and 1930s double-ended bathtubs.

## BED LINENS

**The Linen Works**

www.thelinenworks.co.uk

Pretty French bed linens in 100% washed linen, from pale lavender to deep blue, linen or lambswool throws, and bathroom/home accessories.

**Toast**

www.toast.co.uk

Washed linen and cotton bed linens in soft shades, pure linen sheets, and organic striped designs. Also cushions, wool blankets and sheepskin rugs.

**Volga Linen**
Unit E6 Engineering Offices
The Gasworks
2 Michael Road
London SW6 2AD
(by appointment only)
020 7736 7756

www.volgalinen.co.uk

High quality white bed linens in 100% linen, featuring hemstitch detailing, plus soft coloured crushed linens. Also table and kitchen linens, 100% linen by the metre, and ready made linen curtains.

**The White Company**

www.thewhitecompany.com

An enormous range of quality bed linens, from high-thread-count Egyptian cottons to 100% washed linen. Also bedding, towels, bath accessories and decorative homeware.

## RUGS, CUSHIONS & DECORATIVE ACCESSORIES

**Cox & Cox**

www.coxandcox.co.uk

Online homeware store offering velvet and faux-fur cushions, throws, bean bags, rugs, occasional furniture and decorative accessories.

**Deirdre Dyson**
554 Kings Road
London SW6 2DZ
020 7384 4464

www.deirdredyson.com

Contemporary handmade carpets and rugs, with abstract and organic motifs. Bespoke design service.

**French Connection Home**

www.frenchconnection.com

The fashion chain's chic, pared down homeware collection includes smart but affordable side tables, linen cushions, knitted throws and cool lighting.

**Allegra Hicks**
020 7736 1372

www.allegrahicks.com

Wool and/or silk rugs, decorative cushions, printed linens and cut velvets, plus a range of interiors accessories, all in Allegra Hicks' distinctive modern organic designs and soft colours.

**Niki Jones**

www.niki-jones.co.uk

Online store with modern designs made using craft techniques. Embroidered cushions, bed throws, and hand-knotted wool rugs in distinctive geometric patterns.

**Orla Kiely**
31 Monmouth Street
London WC2H 9DD
020 7240 4022

www.orlakiely.com

Cotton and linen print cushions, throws, bed linens and home accessories, all in this British designer's distinctive organic motifs and strong colours.

**Jennifer Manners**
020 8741 9360

www.jennifermanners.co.uk

Bespoke rugs in graphic, geometric and vintage-inspired designs.

**Tori Murphy**

www.torimurphy.com

British-made own-design lambswool cushions, throws and pouffes, in smart chevrons, over-size dogstooth, stripes and checks. Soft pastels and monochromes.

**Rowen & Wren**

www.rowenandwren.co.uk

Simply styled, beautifully crafted wool and crewelwork cushions, wool blankets, washed bed linens and furniture.

**The Rug Company**
124 Holland Park Avenue,
London W11 4UE
020 7908 9990

www.therugcompany.com

Every style from classic to bold contemporary designs, 'designer' collections and the Studio Collection featuring playful, informal chevron, diamond and harlequin patterns.

**Zara Home**

zarahome.com

Chic, budget high-street cushions in plains and prints, plus home accessories for every room

# US Sources

## ONE-STOP STYLE SHOPS

**ABC Carpet and Home**
888 & 881 Broadway
New York, NY 10003
212 473 3000,

www.abchome.com

Inspirational furniture store with everything for the home, including bed and bath, lighting, furniture and carpets and rugs.

**Crate and Barrel**

www.crateandbarrel.com

Affordable, modern furniture, plus contemporary bed and bath, home accessories and excellent storage solutions.

**Dwell Studio**
77 Wooster Street
New York, NY 10012
646 442 6000,

www.dwellstudio.com

Chic modern furniture, colourful rugs, smart beds and home accessories.

**Jonathan Adler**

www.jonathanadler.com

The designer's colourful graphic designs appear on everything from bath towels and cushions to witty cocktail and side tables, upholstery and bright ceramics.

**Pottery Barn**

www.potterybarn.com

Classic and contemporary furniture, plus home accessories, bed/bath ranges and tabletop.

**Kelly Wearstler**
8440 Melrose Avenue
West Hollywood
CA 90069
323 895 7880

www.kellywearstler.com

The fashion and lifestyle designer has turned her hand to funky graphic wallpapers, furniture, cushions and throws, muted and bright colours.

**Madeline Weinrib**
126 5th Avenue
2nd Floor
New York, NY 10011,
(by appointment only)
212 414 5978

www.madelineweinrib.com

Rugs, cushions and fabrics in a mix of smart chevrons and ikats, featuring cool bright colours. Also jacquards, block prints and embroidery.

## RUGS, CUSHIONS & DECORATIVE ACCESSORIES

**Amy Butler**

www.amybutlerdesign.com

Glorious modern botanical motif 100% wool rugs in zesty colours, plus wallpaper and wall art designs.

**Hable Construction**

www.hableconstruction.com

Hand-printed canvas and linen cushions in modern organic prints, plus smart printed storage boxes.

**Trina Turk**
891 N Palm Canyon Drive
Palm Springs
CA 92262
760 416 2856

www.trinaturk.com

Bright cushions, bed linen and tabletop designs in graphic geometrics and sunny colours.

**Vanderhurd**
5 Crosby Street, No 6B
New York, NY 10013,
212 213 6514

www.vanderhurd.com

Bespoke silk and wool dhurries in bold organic and geometric patterns, carpets, and flatweaves in herringbone and textured plains. Also designer cushions in strong patterns.

## SURFACES

**Ann Sacks**

www.annsacks.com

19 showrooms with an enormous range of porcelain tiles, stone, glass and mosaics, plus patterned speciality stones.

**Artistic Tile**
38 West 21st Street
New York, NY 10010
212 727 9331

www.artistictile.com

A vast selection of tile, glass and stone, plus unusual surfaces such as mother of pearl mosaics and organic carved stone.

**Coverings Etc**

www.coveringsetc.com

A great source of innovative natural stone and mosaics, including terrazzo flooring, recycled coloured glass surfaces, and Bio-luminum, made from recycled aluminium from reclaimed aircraft parts.

**Edelman Leather**
D & D Building
979 3rd Avenue
2nd Floor
New York, NY 10022
212 751 3339,

www.edelmanleather.com

Wonderful upholstery leathers, including crocodile effect and modern metallics, plus wall and floor leather tiles.

**Walking on Wood**
1127 2nd Avenue
New York, NY 10022
212 832 2500

www.walkingonwood.com

Specialist handmade timber parquet flooring in many designs.

## KITCHENS & BATHROOMS

**The Bath Works**

www.thebathworks.com

Bathroom specialists offering an excellent choice of vintage European freestanding bathtub styles, plus restored originals.

**Restoration Hardware**

www.restorationhardware.com

Beautiful bathrooms, plus hardware, furniture, bed linens, decorative items and outdoor furniture.

**Waterworks**

www.waterworks.com

Huge choice of classic and contemporary bathroom and kitchens products, including surfaces from ceramic to concrete and smart bath linens.

**Urban Archeology**
239 East 58th Street
New York, NY 10022
212 371 4646

www.urbanarcheology.com

Freestanding bathtubs based on vintage designs in marble and metal, plus innovative surfaces, including ceramic, stone, glass, cement and metal.

## WALLPAPERS & FABRICS

**Flavor Paper**

www.flavorpaper.com

Brooklyn-based hand-screened wallpapers with super-funky retro and modern prints, unusual colours and finishes, and an Andy Warhol collection. Coordinating cushions, too.

**Grow House Grow**

www.growhousegrow.com

Very quirky, narrative-inspired wallpapers, fabrics and tiles, featuring whimsical prints and unusual colours. Also hand-crafted encaustic tiles; custom colours available.

**Henry Road**
12240 ½ Ventura Boulevard
Studio City, CA 91604
818 762 8966

www.henryroad.com

Super-cool, colourful own-design fabrics featuring bold colours, stripes and modern botanicals, cushions, funky lampshades and also glass tiles featuring their designs.

**Hygge and West**

www.hyggeandwest.com

Very cool designer wallpapers in whimsical and modern organic patterns and unusual colourways. Removable wallpaper tiles to match.

**Spoonflower**

www.spoonflower.com

Quirky, graphic and fun wallpapers and fabrics, plus an online facility to print your own custom designs on fabric and wallpaper.

**Studio Bon Textiles**

www.studiobontextiles.com

Bonnee Sharp's beautiful own-design hand-printed textiles include etchy florals, geometrics and funky graphics, all in a fresh palette. Customized colourization available.

**Walnut Wallpaper**
7424 Beverly Boulevard
Los Angeles
CA 90036,
323 932 9166

www.walnutwallpaper.com

Huge selection of designer wallpapers, available to view online according to colour groups or style categories such as Retro, Foil or Architectural.

# PICTURE CREDITS

**2** Judith Kramer, owner of webshop Juudt.com; the art of living; living and art; **3** The home of the interior designer Sarah Lavoine in Paris; **4–5** The home of the designer Emma Oldham of Solange Design, London; **6** The home of the interior designer Sarah Lavoine in Paris; **7** The family home of Melanie Ireland, founder and creator of Simple Kids, Antwerp; **8 left** Michela Imperiali www.MIKinteriors.com; **8 right** The home of the interior decorator Caroline Van Thillo in Belgium; **9** The family home of Sacha Paisley in Sussex, designed by Arior Design; **10** and **11 right** The home of the decorator Bunny Turner of www.turnerpocock.co.uk; **11 left** The home of the interior decorator Caroline Van Thillo in Belgium; **12–13** L'Atelier d'Archi – Isabelle Juy – www.latelierdarchi.fr; **14** Judith Kramer, owner of webshop Juudt.com; the art of living; living and art; **15** A family home in Islington designed by Nicola Harding; **16** The home of family Voors in the Netherlands designed by Karin Draaijer; **17** The home of the interior designer Sarah Lavoine in Paris; **18 left** Long Farm: The home of architect Lucy Marston in Suffolk; **18 right** The home of the interior decorator Caroline Van Thillo in Belgium; **19** The home of the decorator Bunny Turner of www.turnerpocock.co.uk; **20** The family home of Melanie Ireland, founder and creator of Simple Kids, Antwerp; **21** Judith Kramer, owner of webshop Juudt.com; the art of living; living and art; **22** The home of Victoria and Stephen Fordham, designed by Sarah Delaney, in London; **23 left** The home of the designer Anne Geistdoerfer (and her family) of double g architects in Paris; **23 right** The family home of Melanie Ireland, founder and creator of Simple Kids, Antwerp; **24** The home of the decorator Bunny Turner of www.turnerpocock.co.uk; **25** Michela Imperiali www.MIKinteriors.com; **26** The home of the interior decorator Caroline Van Thillo in Belgium; **27** Michela Imperiali www.MIKinteriors.com; **28 left** The home of the interior decorator Caroline Van Thillo in Belgium; **28 right** The family home of Sacha Paisley in Sussex, designed by Arior Design; **29** The home of the interior designer Sarah Lavoine in Paris; **30–31** L'Atelier d'Archi – Isabelle Juy – www.latelierdarchi.fr; **32–33** The family home of Sacha Paisley in Sussex, designed by Arior Design; **34–35** Judith Kramer, owner of webshop Juudt.com; the art of living; living and art; **36–37** Long Farm: The home of architect Lucy Marston in Suffolk; **38–39** L'Atelier d'Archi – Isabelle Juy – www.latelierdarchi.fr; **40** Michela Imperiali www.MIKinteriors.com; **41** The home of the designer Emma Oldham of Solange Design, London; **42–43** Judith Kramer, owner of webshop Juudt.com; the art of living; living and art; **44–45** The home of the designer Anne Geistdoerfer (and her family) of double g architects in Paris; **46–47** The home of the interior decorator Caroline Van Thillo in Belgium; **48** A family home in Islington designed by Nicola Harding; **49–50** The home of the interior decorator Caroline Van Thillo in Belgium; **51** The home of the interior designer Sarah Lavoine in Paris; **52–53** The home of the decorator Bunny Turner of www.turnerpocock.co.uk; **54–55** Judith Kramer, owner of webshop Juudt.com; the art of living; living and art; **56–57** The home of the designer Emma Oldham of Solange Design, London; **58** A family home in Islington designed by Nicola Harding; **59** The home of the designer Anne Geistdoerfer (and her family) of double g architects in Paris; **60–61** The home of the interior designer Sarah Lavoine in Paris; **62** The home of the interior decorator Caroline Van Thillo in Belgium; **63** The home of the interior designer Sarah Lavoine in Paris; **64–65** The home of the decorator Bunny Turner of www.turnerpocock.co.uk; **66** The home of family Voors in the Netherlands designed by Karin Draaijer; **67** The family home of Melanie Ireland, founder and creator of Simple Kids, Antwerp; **68** L'Atelier d'Archi – Isabelle Juy – www.latelierdarchi.fr; **69** Judith Kramer, owner of webshop Juudt.com; the art of living; living and art; **70** The home of the designer Emma Oldham of Solange Design, London; **71–72** The home of family Voors in the Netherlands designed by Karin Draaijer; **73 left** The family home of Sacha Paisley in Sussex, designed by Arior Design; **73 right** The home of family Voors in the Netherlands designed by Karin Draaijer; **74–75** The home of the interior decorator Caroline Van Thillo in Belgium; **76** The home of the decorator Bunny Turner of www.turnerpocock.co.uk; **77** Judith Kramer, owner of webshop Juudt.com; the art of living; living and art; **78** The home of the interior decorator Caroline Van Thillo in Belgium; **79** The family home of Sacha Paisley in Sussex, designed by Arior Design; **80–81** The home of the interior decorator Caroline Van Thillo in Belgium; **82–83** Long Farm: The home of architect Lucy Marston in Suffolk; **84** The home of the interior designer Sarah Lavoine in Paris; **85** Judith Kramer, owner of webshop Juudt.com; the art of living; living and art; **86–87** L'Atelier d'Archi – Isabelle Juy – www.latelierdarchi.fr; **88** The home of the designer Emma Oldham of Solange Design, London; **89** The home of the decorator Bunny Turner of www.turnerpocock.co.uk; **90–91** The home of family Voors in the Netherlands designed by Karin Draaijer; **92–93** Michela Imperiali www.MIKinteriors.com; **94** The home of the designer Anne Geistdoerfer (and her family) of double g architects in Paris; **95 left** and **above right** The family home of Melanie Ireland, founder and creator of Simple Kids, Antwerp; **95 below right** The home of the designer Anne Geistdoerfer (and her family) of double g architects in Paris; **96** A family home in Islington designed by Nicola Harding; **97** Long Farm: The home of architect Lucy Marston in Suffolk; **98–99** The home of the decorator Bunny Turner of www.turnerpocock.co.uk; **100–101** The home of the interior designer Sarah Lavoine in Paris; **102–103** The home of Victoria and Stephen Fordham, designed by Sarah Delaney, in London; **104–107** A family home in Islington designed by Nicola Harding; **108–109** The home of the designer Emma Oldham of Solange Design, London; **110–111** Long Farm: The home of architect Lucy Marston in Suffolk; **112–113** The family home of Sacha Paisley in Sussex, designed by Arior Design; **114–115** The home of Victoria and Stephen Fordham, designed by Sarah Delaney, in London; **116–117** Judith Kramer, owner of webshop Juudt.com; the art of living; living and art; **118–119** Long Farm: The home of architect Lucy Marston in Suffolk; **120–121 left** L'Atelier d'Archi – Isabelle Juy – www.latelierdarchi.fr; **121 right** The home of family Voors in the Netherlands designed by Karin Draaijer; **122–123** The home of the designer Anne Geistdoerfer (and her family) of double g architects in Paris; **124–125** The home of the decorator Bunny Turner of www.turnerpocock.co.uk; **126** The family home of Sacha Paisley in Sussex, designed by Arior Design; **127** L'Atelier d'Archi – Isabelle Juy – www.latelierdarchi.fr; **128–129** The home of Victoria and Stephen Fordham, designed by Sarah Delaney, in London; **130–131** Long Farm: The home of architect Lucy Marston in Suffolk; **132–133** The home of the designer Anne Geistdoerfer (and her family) of double g architects in Paris**; 134–135** Judith Kramer, owner of webshop Juudt.com; the art of living; living and art; **136–137** The family home of Sacha Paisley in Sussex, designed by Arior Design; **138** Judith Kramer, owner of webshop Juudt.com; the art of living; living and art; **139** The home of the interior decorator Caroline Van Thillo in Belgium; **140–141** A family home in Islington designed by Nicola Harding;**142** Michela Imperiali www.MIKinteriors.com; **143** The home of the interior decorator Caroline Van Thillo in Belgium; **144–145** The home of the designer Anne Geistdoerfer (and her family) of double g architects in Paris; **146–147 above left** L'Atelier d'Archi – Isabelle Juy – www.latelierdarchi.fr; **147 below centre** and **right** Long Farm: The home of architect Lucy Marston in Suffolk; **148** Michela Imperiali www.MIKinteriors.com; **149 above right** Long Farm: The home of architect Lucy Marston in Suffolk; **149 below left** The home of the designer Anne Geistdoerfer (and her family) of double g architects in Paris; **150 left** and **right** The home of the designer Anne Geistdoerfer (and her family) of double g architects in Paris; **150 centre** The home of the interior designer Sarah Lavoine in Paris; **151** The family home of Melanie Ireland, founder and creator of Simple Kids, Antwerp.

# BUSINESS CREDITS

**SARAH DELANEY INTERIORS**

E: info@sarahdelaneydesign.co.uk
T: + 44 (0) 20 7221 2010
www.sarahdelaneydesign.co.uk

**Pages 22, 102–103, 114–115, 128–129.**

**KARIN DRAAIJER**

***Interieurontwerper***
Draaijer Bvba
Fabriekstraat 149a
B-3950 Kalille
Belgium
T: +32 (0)494 754070
www.karindraaijer.com

**Pages 16, 66, 71–72, 73 right, 90–91, 121 right.**

**ANNE GEISTDOERFER**

***Architectes***
www.doubleg.fr

**Pages 23 left, 44–45, 59, 94, 95 below right, 122–123, 132–133, 144–145, 149 below left; 150.**

**NICOLA HARDING**

***Interior & Garden Design***
116 Percy Road
London W12 9QB
T: +44 (0)208 743 6690
M: +44 (0)7989 963 647
www.nicolaharding.com

**Pages 15, 48, 58, 96, 104–107, 140–141.**

**MICHELA IMPERIALI**

www.MIKinteriors.com

**Pages 8 left, 25, 27, 40, 92–93, 142, 148.**

**ISABELLE JUY**

***L'Atelier d'Archi***
www.latelierdarchi.fr

**Pages 12–13, 30–31, 38–39, 68, 86–87, 120, 121 left, 127, 146, 147 above left.**

**JUDITH KRAMER**

www.juudt.com

**Pages 2, 14, 21, 34–35, 42–43, 54–55, 69, 77, 85, 116–117, 134–135, 138.**

**SARAH LAVOINE**

***Studio d'Architecture Interieure***
205 rue Saint Honoré
75001 Paris
France
T: +33 (0)1 42 60 60 40
www.sarahlavoine.com

**Pages 3, 6, 17, 29, 51, 60–61, 63, 84, 100–101, 150 centre.**

**LUCY MARSTON ARCHITECTS**

www.lucymarston.com

**Pages 18 left, 36–37, 82–83, 97, 110–111, 118–119, 130–131, 147 below centre, 147 right, 149 above right,**

**EMMA OLDHAM**

***Solange Design***
3-5 Barrett Street
3rd Floor West
London W1U 1AY
T: +44 (0)20 3005 5472
www.solangedesign.com

**Pages 4–5, 41, 56–57, 70, 88, 108–109.**

**SIMPLE KIDS**

Head Office
T: +32 (0)3 257 1682
www.simplekids.be

**Pages 7, 20, 23 right, 67, 95 left, 95 above right, 151.**

**CATHERINE SMITH**

Interior Designer/Director
***Arior Design***
Studio 2
20 Regent Street
Brighton BN1 1UX
T: 01273 579931
E: info@ariordesign.co.uk
www.ariordesign.co.uk

**Pages 9, 28 right, 32–33, 73 left, 79, 112–113, 126, 136–137.**

**BUNNY TURNER**

***Turner Pocock Interior Design***
Unit 18A
First Floor Parsons Green Depot
Parsons Green Lane
London SW6 4HH
T: +44 203 463 2390

and

3, Route de Geneve
1260 Nyon
Switzerland
T: + 41 7919 27558
http://turnerpocock.co.uk

**Pages 10, 11 right, 19, 24, 52–53, 64–65, 76, 89, 98–99, 124–125.**

**CAROLINE VAN THILLO**

Interior Decorator
***MJL-Interiors***
Bredabaan 158
2930 Brasschaat
Belgium
T: +32 (0)3 653 5596
Facebook:
MJL-Interiors by Caroline Van Thillo

**Pages 8 right, 11 left, 18 right, 26, 28 left, 46–47, 49–50, 62, 74–75,78, 80- 81, 139, 143.**

# INDEX

Figures in *italics* indicate captions.

# ACKNOWLEDGMENTS

Working on a book like this is an enormous team effort. So thank you, Polly Wreford, for taking such amazing photographs, for your wonderful artistic eye and for being such fun. Thank you to Annabel Morgan for being a simply brilliant editor, to Jess Walton for sourcing spot-on locations and to Paul Tilby for a dynamic and very stylish book design.

Thanks also to Cindy Richards and Leslie Harrington for giving *Think Home* the green light, and to Fiona Lindsay at Limelight Celebrity Management for her continued support. Thank you to all the designers, architects and owners who so very kindly allowed us to photograph their homes, and for their expert words of wisdom.

And thank you Anthony, Cicely and Felix, for all your encouragement, cups of tea and simply being there. *Think Home* is about creating a beautiful, practical space – but it's the people at home who matter the most.